THE NALGAP ANNOTATED BIBLIOGRAPHY:

Resources on Alcoholism, Substance Abuse, and Lesbians/Gay Men

Steven L. Berg
Dana Finnegan
Emily McNally

Fort Wayne

The National Association of
Lesbian and Gay Alcoholism Professionals

1987

National Association of
Lesbian and Gay Alcoholism Professionals

Published by the National Association of
Lesbian and Gay Alcoholism Professionals

1208 E. State Blvd.
Fort Wayne, IN 468095

Cover Design
Harvey E. Ballard, Jr.

ANDREW P. STUART

friend, mentor, confidant

--Steven L. Berg

TO OUR FAMILIES

whose love and support have helped us
to live our lives with dignity and pride

--Dana Finnegan
Emily McNally

CONTENTS

ACKNOWLEDGEMENTS

Although the NALGAP Annotated Bibliography: Alcoholism, Substance Abuse, and Lesbians/Gay Men is the first attempt to gather and to fully annotate all materials which have been written on this topic, it is also the fourth edition of the NALGAP Bibliography. As a result of this unique situation, two sets of acknowledgements are called for. The following people were directly responsible for helping us produce the book which you now hold.

Because we live in a less than perfect world, we need to mention that affiliation with this research implies nothing about a person's sexual orientation. NALGAP is grateful for the support of our non-lesbian and non-gay colleagues and wishes to acknowledge that this bibliography could not have been produced without their help.

The National Association of Lesbian and Gay Alcoholism Professionals, the Funding Exchange/National Community Funds, Lillian Spinning, LeClair Bissell, and Larry Siegel provided financial assistance.

Ron Vachon helped coordinate the printing for the book.

Jannette Fiore and Anne Tracy in Special Collections at Michigan State University's library guided me as I worked with alternative (meaning unindexed) materials. Without Michael Bennett's help with interlibrary loans, I couldn't have verified many of these citations.

During her sabbatical year, Mary Schneider allowed me to use her office which I designated as the bibliography headquarters. Cathy Davidson and George Landon have been major influences on my academic and professional life. My gratitude to them involves much more than their assistance with this book.

Valerie Przywara, Jack Ryan, Dwight James, Tim Jed, Craig Bernthal, Harvey Ballard, Barbara Harte, and Elizabeth Thompson gave encouragement and support.

Christopher Bargeron, Karl Hatop, Thom DeVoogd, Mark DeRuiter, and Jonathan Kennedy worked as research assistants.

All people should have someone like Rachel "Grandma" Liberacki in their life. I'm blessed to have her unconditional love, constant support and encouragement, and fine example as part of my daily experience.

Andrew Stuart shared his expertise as a librarian, humored me when I was tired, covered expenses when I was short on cash, listened to me complain when I was frustrated, and generally served as a friend, mentor, and confidant. Andrew frequently remains quietly in the background, but without his constant support, I couldn't have maintained enough serenity to actually complete this project.

Steven L. Berg, M.A.
East Lansing, MI
18 April 1987

ACKNOWLEDGEMENTS

We want to thank the following people for their invaluable contributions. Without their help, we would have been unable to gather the core materials which served as a basis for the original NALGAP Bibliography. In addition, these people helped establish a climate where the issue of alcoholism and substance abuse in the lesbian and gay community could be safely discussed in professional circles.

Nancy Tucker and Cade Ware were pioneers in presenting information to counselors at the Rutgers Summer School of Alcohol Studies. They were among the first to share their experiences with professionals who were seeking assistance and guidance in treating their lesbian and gay clients. In addition, Nancy Tucker kept files of unpublished papers that people sent to her at her request and of newspaper clippings about working with lesbian/gay alcoholics. When we started the National Association of Lesbian and Gay Alcoholism Professionals, she turned all of her files over to us, and it was the contents of these files which formed the core of the NALGAP archives and of the first and subsequent NALGAP bibliographies.

In the mid-1970's, at a time when most people were afraid to say the word "lesbian," Brenda Weathers spoke out and wrote an article about alcoholism among lesbians. Her courage helped to break the conspiracy of silence.

Tom Ziebold also helped break the conspiracy of silence. In the mid-1970's, he spoke out via two influential articles on gays, alcoholism, and recovery. He also did workshops and presented papers at conferences on lesbian/gay alcoholism and, along with John Mongeon, edited the first collection of papers on alcoholism and the lesbian/gay community.

The mid-1970's produced another pioneer--Lillene Fifield. She did the first research study of the incidence of alcoholism among lesbians and gay men and of the alcoholism treatment they received. This study is frequently referred to in the alcoholism field, and it certainly revealed the desperate need for better treatment for lesbian and gay male alcoholics.

Tom Smith, MD, also has contributed greatly to the literature and to the field. He has written many articles on alcoholism and gays and wrote several of the first articles on the connection between chemical addiction and AIDS. In addition, Tom supported NALGAP's earliest efforts at making literature available by allowing NALGAP to print one of his articles and to keep the proceeds. His generosity helped finance the first bibliography.

George Marcelle's efforts at the National Council on Alcoholism helped bring about the first "track" of presentation on lesbian and gay alcoholism at the 1980 NCA Forum on Alcoholism which was held in Seattle. This track created a central forum for presentors and generated a large number of significant papers which were then made available via the first bibliography.

Bill Cohen, publisher of Haworth Press, has helped to create a safer environment for publications such as the _NALGAP Annotated Bibliography_ by publishing the _Journal of Homosexuality_. In 1982, Haworth Press published the first edited collection of articles, _Alcoholism and Homosexuality_ as a volume of the _Journal of Homosexuality_. In addition, he has consistently encouraged NALGAP's efforts.

By her publication of the lesbian and gay counseling

bibliographies and by her courage in coming out in an earlier, more hostile time, Barbara Gittings inspired us to publish the first NALGAP Bibliography.

Jack Ryan, Co-President of NALGAP, has helped the organization grow and flourish. His support and dedication have made it possible for NALGAP to expand its publication efforts. Without his effective leadership, NALGAP would not have been in a position to publish this manuscript.

LeClair Bissell shared her knowledge and experience and encouraged and supported our efforts.

Ellen Ratner has consistently supported NALGAP's efforts to expand and publish this new bibliography. Her support has helped make it possible.

In the final analysis, it is Steven Berg's hard work, dedication, and expertise that have expanded this bibliography into a full-fledged professional publication.

Dana Finnegan, Ph.D., CAC
Emily McNally, M.Ed., CAC
New York, NY
30 March 1987

WHAT IS NALGAP?

The National Association of Lesbian and Gay Alcoholism Professionals (NALGAP) is a non-profit, tax exempt organization dedicated to three major goals:

1. Forming a network of communication and support for lesbian and gay addiction professionals.

2. Improving treatment for lesbian and gay chemically addicted clients.

3. Assisting chemical dependency agencies and all helping treatment professionals to better serve their lesbian and gay clients.

The membership is composed of counselors, nurses, physicians, social workers, psychologists, members of AA and Alanon, drug and alcohol agencies and institutions as well as lesbian and gay organizations and concerned citizens throughout the world.

NALGAP publishes a quarterly newsletter, a bibliography, and a directory of facilities and services which claim to be sensitive to lesbian and gay issues in addictions therapy. Through the office for the bibliography, we make available to students, reserchers, and other interested persons articles and unpublished papers on homosexuality and chemical dependency.

The Education Committee provides, thorugh the talent of many members, workshops and seminars as well as in-service training programs to help treatment personnel recognize and deal with the specific problems facing sexual minorities.

The support offered to members, especially in areas with little or no lesbian and gay community activity, is extremely valuable. To those professionals who must remain closeted at work, having others with whom they may correspond is often ver comforting. Therefore, NALGAP provides a Confidential Directory of members who have granted permission to be listed.

In 1985, NALGAP began a schedule of bi-annual national conferences to enable persons interested in the issues of lesbian and gay alcoholism and substance abuse to share, to hear knowledgeable speakers, to have an input into the association, and to offer encouragement and support to each other.

We hope through this bibliography to make NALGAP better known. And we hope that you will consider becoming an active member.

Jack Ryan, MA
Fraelean Curtis, LICSW
NALGAP Co-Presidents

INTRODUCTION

A Short History

In 1979, Dana Finnegan and Emily McNally co-founded the National Association of Lesbian and Gay Alcoholism Professionals. At that time they had the dream of compiling a list of resources for people working in the field of chemical addiction and for writers and researchers who could not find materials on this subject. The following year, NALGAP published a bibliography on alcoholism in the lesbian and gay community. It was updated in 1981 and 1983.

In 1985, as part of his work as co-chair of Dignity Region 5's Substance Abuse Task Force, Steve Berg began compiling an annotated bibliography on homosexuality and chemical addiction. While doing research on this project he was "introduced" to Dana and Emily through the bibliography they had written for NALGAP. Steve, Dana, and Emily met face-to-face at NALGAP's first national conference held in Chicago in September, 1985.

During the NALGAP business meeting which followed the conference, the need to update the NALGAP resource list was addressed. At that time, with the approval of the newly formed board of directors, the Finnegan/McNally bibliography and the Berg bibliography were combined to form the NALGAP Annotated Bibliography: Resources on Alcoholism, Substance Abuse, and Lesbians/Gay Men.

During the following year, work on the bibliography was coordinated between the Dana and Emily's New York office and Steve's office at Michigan State University. Working in New York, Dana and Emily copied, sorted, and organized the many unpublished manuscripts which they had gathered during the past seven years. At MSU, Steve organized bibliographic research necessary not only to update, but to expand the bibliography which NALGAP had previously published.

As a result of this collaboration, the 300 unannotated citations grew into this this book which includes over 900 fully annotated citations.

Types of Material Gathered

The NALGAP Annotated Bibliography is the first attempt to compile everything that has been published and written concerning chemical addiction in the lesbian and gay community. If a book, article, brochure, pamphlet, conference paper, dissertation, thesis, or manuscript mentioned lesbians or gay men and some type(s) of chemical addiction, we included it in the bibliography. And, to the best of his ability, Steve has annotated each entry without bias or commentary. He simply wanted to record what was available and how to get it.

The authors are also aware that many treatment professionals who want to provide quality services to their lesbian and gay clients might not know much about homosexuality. Furthermore, many lesbians and gay men, when they are first coming out, do not know where they might gather materials to learn about themselves. For these people, a selected bibliography on homosexuality has been included.

Because the rate of alcoholism in the lesbian and gay community is between 24-40%, people working to address the needs of lesbians and gay men will want to educate themselves about chemical addiction. Also, the lesbian or gay man who comes to the realization that she or he has an alcohol or drug problem might not know what printed resources are available to them. For these individuals, a selected bibliography on chemical addiction will be found in this book.

In choosing books for the two selected bibliographies it was not possible to list everything. Only best and most available books in those fields were included. Individuals who desire more information about some aspect of homosexuality or chemical addiction should consult one of the bibliographies which have been listed. And, such individuals should be aware that many of the books which are included in the selected bibliographies include selected bibliographies of their own.

Style and Vocabulary

Citations basically follow the style manual of the Modern Language Association. Exceptions include those sources where our information was either incomplete or came to us from a source that used some other style.

Vocabulary in both the field of chemical addiction and homosexuality is politically charged. In this bibliography, "homosexual" refers to men and women, "gay" usually refers to men, and "lesbian" refers to women. "Alcoholism" refers to alcohol abuse and "substance abuse" refers to abuse of drugs other than alcohol. "Chemical addiction/dependency" refers to both alcohol and drug abuse. Exceptions include those passages we have lifted directly from the text.

Unpublished Papers

Many of the unpublished papers and manuscripts are available through the National Association of Lesbian and Gay Alcoholism Professionals. For a small charge, where NALGAP has the author's permission to do so, the organization can duplicate these papers and send them to individuals who are interested in them. NALGAP is also able to provide some limited bibliographic help to individuals working in this area. Requests for papers and bibliographic questions should be sent to NALGAP's New York office which is located at 204 West 20th Street, New York, NY 10011.

In order for us to continue to provide the best resources possible in the field, please send up copies of articles which you were disappointed not to find in this bibliography

RESOURCES ON ALCOHOLISM, SUBSTANCE ABUSE,

AND LESBIANS/GAY MEN

In this section of the NALGAP Annotated Bibliography we have attempted to list everything that has been published or written concerning alcoholism and substance abuse in the lesbian and gay community. Sources listed in this section include books, articles, conference papers, dissertations, thesises, and unpublished manuscripts. In those cases where we have been unable to locate the material we have cited, we list the source of our information.

001 A. "Fall Journal." Out From Under. Ed. Jean Swallow. San Francisco: Spinsters, Ink, 1983. 11-24.

"A." recounts her struggle with addiction and staying sober. The reader can feel her anxiety of wishing to get high on heroin and her disappointment once she does.

002 Abbott, Sidney and Barbara Love. Sappho Was a Right-On Woman. 1972. New York: Stein and Day, 1973.

In the introduction, the authors write that it is not lesbianism that makes lesbians prone to suicide and alcoholism but "it is the self-degradation our society went to pains to teach us..."

003 Abraham, Karl. "The Psychological Relations Between Sexuality and Alcoholism." International Journal of Psychoanalysis 7 (1926): 2-10.

Abraham finds that: "The expressions of feeling which...were branded as morbid or immoral may be observed...whenever men are drinking heavily; and every drinking bout is tinged with homosexuality." Examples are cited.

004 Achilles, Nancy. "The Development of the Homosexual Bar as an Institution." _Sexual Deviance._ Ed. J. Gagnon and W. Simon. New York: Harper and Row, 1967: 228-42.

This dated article focuses on San Francisco.

005 d'Adesky, Anne-Christine. "Alcohol, Drugs, and Gays." _New York Native_ 24 March 1986: 15.

A summary of "10% of Those We Serve," a conference on alcoholism in the homosexual community which was sponsored by the New York City Department of Health. Special focus is given to Dana Finnegan and Edward Ellis' "Lesbian and Gay Males--Adult Children of Alcoholism."

006 Adkins, Barry. "Liquor May Be Quicker, But Pride is Just Dandy: Two Lesbians Open a Chemical Dependency Treatment Center for Gays." _New York Native_ 19 May 1986: 18.

The article describes Pride Institute, the first treatment facility designed around the needs of lesbian/gay clients.

007 Aggie, et al. _What are You Doing in the Closet?_ Los Angeles: Alcoholism Center for Women, nd.

The authors write that: "Our purpose in creating this brochure is to increase lesbian awareness of the disease of alcoholism and how it relates directly from our oppression. There is a direct relationship between lesbianism and alcoholism; however, to be a lesbian does not mean one is an alcoholic." With increased awareness of alcoholism, lesbians will be able to "Come Out...Sober!"

008 "Al-Anon is for Gay People, Too." Al-Anon Faces Alcoholism. New York: Al-Anon Family Group Headquarters, 1965. 160-63.

A gay man tells his story.

009 Al-Anon Faces Alcoholism. New York: Al-Anon Family Group Headquarters, 1965.

The book includes "Al-Anon is for Gay People, Too."

010 "Alcohol: What It Is And What It Does." Advocate 25 February 1974: 20-21.

A general essay on alcohol that includes a chart of how alcohol affects various parts of the body.

011 "Alcohol, Drugs, and AIDS--What's the Connection?" NAGAP Newsletter 5.3 (1984): 2-3.

A brief survey of information about alcohol and drugs as co-factors for the development of AIDS.

012 "The Alcoholic Homosexual." CAFC Newsletter June 1979.

A general discussion as to how treatment professionals can meet the needs of the homosexual client.

013 "Alcoholism." Mandate: The International Magazine of Entertainment and Eros 6.69 (1981): 30-2+.

The author combines statistical information, comments from alcoholism professionals, professional studies, and personal observations in this well researched and well written presentation.

014 "Alcoholism: Out of the Closet." PLGTF Bulletin 3.9 (September 1981).

A special feature of PLGTF Bulletin which includes Mary O'Donnell's "Alcoholism and Co-Alcoholism," Thomas

Ziebold's "Alcoholism and Recovery," Edward M. Diehl's "Treatment for Lesbians and Gay Men," "Alcoholism Center for Women, Los Angeles, CA," "NAGAP Promotes Services to Gays," "Gay Male Alcoholism Prevention," and Mary Cochran's "Alcoholism."

015 "Alcoholism: Symptoms of Progress." RFD 28 (1981): 28.

The article is obviously reprinted from somewhere, but no source is given. It includes information on the four stages of alcoholism and answers the questions of "What constitutes recovery?" and "What About Relapses?"

016 "Alcoholism and You: A Self Examination." Unitarian Universalist Lesbian/Gay Word April/May 1983: 8.

Standard 26 question self examination.

017 "Alcoholism Center for Women, Los Angeles, CA." PLGTF Bulletin 3.9 (1981): 17.

General description of Los Angeles' Alcoholism Center for Women.

018 "Alcoholism Defined." Unitarian Universalist Lesbian/Gay Word April/May 1983: 7.

A brief overview of alcoholism. Homosexuality is not specifically discussed.

019 "Alcoholism in Our Community." RFD .28 (1981): 25.

In this essay which introduces the special feature on alcoholism, the author points out that: "At a time when we need to gather our individual and collective strength, alcoholism stands in our way."

020 "Alcoholism in the Gay Community." The Sentinel 6 March-17 April 1981.

A four part series focusing on alcoholism, co-alcoholism, couples, and where the alcoholic and co-alcoholic can get help. See "Alcoholism in the Gay Community [Part 4]," "A Tale of Two Couples," "Michael's Story," and "Laurel's Story."

021 "Alcoholism in the Gay Community [Part 4]." The Sentinel 17 April 1981: 4.

This article focuses on where alcoholics and co-alcoholics can receive help in the San Francisco area. A summary of Liliene Fifield's research is also given.

022 Aldrich, Adrian. "Sobering Thoughts." Out From Under. Ed. Jean Swallow. San Francisco: Spinsters, Ink, 1983. 152-60.

Aldrich's story of recovery focuses on a number of issues such as anger, fear, and acceptance. She also discusses her reaction of coming to AA as a lesbian feminist.

023 Alexander, Matthew [pseud]. "Spirit and the Forms of Love: A Homosexual Experience." Nazareth College, 16 March 1985.

In this personal discussion of the forms of love in the homosexual community, Alexander claims his own understanding of love began when he stopped drinking and joined AA. He tells how a combination of Dignity and AA helped him learn how to love God by serving his neighbor.

024 "All About AIDS." Gay Community News 26 February 1983: 11.

This article is cited under the category "Drug Education" in The Alternative Press Index 15.1 (1983): 24.

025 Allec, John. "Drugs: Changing Your Mind." Body Politic 98 (1983): 31-5.

Allec uses Andrew Weil's Chocolate to Morphine: Understanding Mind Active Drugs (Houghton Mifflin) as the starting point for a discussion of various drugs. Physiological and legal aspects of drug use are included.

026 Allen, Clifford. "The Aging Homosexual." The "Third Sex." Ed. Isadore Rubin. New York: New Book, 1966. 91-5.

Allen writes that: "Many homosexuals, unable to find partners, resort to alcohol....The 'drinking homosexual' is one of the most hopeless aspects of the whole problem; he often does not wish to be cured of alcoholism." In his research Allen found that in almost every case where an "invert gets into trouble publicly there is a history of drinking just before."

027 ---. "Homosexuality: Its Nature, Causation, and Treatment." The Problem of Homosexuality Ed. Charles Berg and Clifford Allen. New York: Citadel, 1958.

Allen writes that the homosexual "often tries to drown his miseries in alcohol, although there are usually deeper reasons for his drinking.... Alcoholic psychoses are usually characterized by ideas of persecution and sometimes reveal the underlying homosexual wishes." (55)

028 Altman, Dennis. Homosexual Oppression and Liberation. New York: Avon, 1973.

Altman writes that: "The [homosexual] counterculture is, of course, associated with the widespread use of drugs, though not, I would argue, to the extent that this association is usually made in the press." Specific comments are made about LSD.

029 Ambramson, Mark. "Loving an Alcoholic." Christopher Street 4.1 (1979): 15-7.

Ambramson discusses his relationship with an alcoholic lover and its eventual breakup. See Robert J. Arnold's "Loving an Alcoholic" for a response.

030 Anant, Santokh S. "Former Alcoholics and Social Drinking." Canadian Psychologist 9 (1968): 35.

Anant reports a case study that suggests that an alcoholic might lose his/her sensitivity to alcohol and may return to social drinking. The case involves a gay man.

031 ---. "The Use of Verbal Aversion (Negative Conditioning) With an Alcoholic: A Case Report." Behavior Research and Therapy 6 (1968): 395-96.

A case study of a gay alcoholic who stopped drinking for 23 months after aversion therapy. He now drinks less frequently and in smaller quantities than before therapy.

032 Anderson, Craig L. "Males as Sexual Assault Victims: Multiple Levels of Trauma." Journal of Homosexuality 7.2/3 (1982): 145-62.

Anderson writes that: "Victims [of sexual assault] may abuse alcohol and other chemicals." The article includes a good bibliography on male sexual assault victims.

033 Anderson, M. "Boston's Homeless Gays." Gay Community News 20 September 1980: 10.

The article is listed under the "Alcoholism" category in The Alternative Press Index 12.3 (1980): 2.

034 Anderson, Sandra C. and Donna C. Henderson. "Working with Lesbian Alcoholics." Social Work (November/December 1985): 518-25.

"This article...will examine alcohol problems among lesbians. Specific areas to be discussed include the incidence and prevalence of alcohol problems among lesbians, lesbian identity and experience, the relationship between lesbianism and alcoholism, and treatment strategies and issues. Finally, recommendations concerning the research and treatment needs of this group will be offered.

035 Anthony, Bronwyn D. "Lesbian Client-Lesbian Therapist: Opportunities and Challenges in Working Together." Journal of Homosexuality 7.2/3 (1978): 45-57.

Anthony cites Dimond and Wilsnack's "Alcoholism Among Lesbians" and claims that "more research is required to extend their tentative conclusions."

036 Anderson, Scott. "Beating the Bottle the Gay Way." Advocate 28 June 1979: 25+.

The article is based on an interview with Dave Steward, Director of the Pearl Project, an outreach program to homosexuals with drinking problems. Initially, the article discusses the Pearl Project. It ends with a general discussion of alcoholism recovery. One insight offered is that "Drinkers who aren't in control of their lives are often not dealing with their sexuality either."

037 Arnold, Cathy. "Refrain." Out From Under. Ed. Jean Swallow. San Francisco: Spinsters, Ink, 1983. 151.

A poem of recovery.

038 ---. "Untitled." Out From Under. Ed. Jean Swallow. San Francisco: Spinsters, Ink, 1983. 147.

A poem of recovery.

039 Arnold, Robert J. "Loving an Alcoholic: A Response." Christopher Street 4.8 (1980): 7-9.

Arnold addresses a number of actions Mark Ambramson writes about in his "Loving an Alcoholic;" actions which could lead the reader to a misunderstanding of alcoholism and what can be done to help alcoholics recover. He criticizes Ambramson for not even attempting to find anything out about the disease.

040 Arobateau, Red. "Confessions of a Not-So-Ex-Alcoholic." Lesbian Contradiction: A Journal of Irreverent Feminism 6 (1983): 18-20.

Arobateau tells how she improved her life by not drinking only to begin after nine years of sobriety. She then tells about coming back to sobriety a second time. Of particular interest is that her last drinking binge--which lasted for over a year--began with Nyquil. The article was reprinted on pages 161-69 of Jean Swallow's Out From Under.

041 Artz, Joan. "Can Minorities Be Invisible: If Not, Why Not?" American Journal of Drug and Alcohol Abuse 3.1 (1976): 181-83.

Artz comments on recent findings that nurses consider "drug addicts, alcoholics, criminals, attempted suicides, very old people, homosexuals, welfare patients, and those viewed as minority group members" to be distasteful patients.

042 Austin, L. "Alcoholism and Gay Youth." Gay Community News 21 February 1981: 8.

The article is cited in The Alternative Press Index 13.1 (1981): 2.

043 B., L. "In Diversity is Strength." Box 1980 ["The Grapevine"] April 1982: 18-9.

L.B. shares "some subjective impressions of the 1981 Illinois State [AA] Conference;" impressions which focus around the gay hospitality suite.

044 B., N. "Chemical Dependency in the Gay Community." Gay Community News 7 April 1984: 5.

N.B. discusses chemical dependency in terms of a "gay plague" and gives some of his/her drug history.

045 B., S. "Condemned to Live an Underground Life." Box 1980 ["The Grapevine"] (July 1976): 32-5.

S.B. tells about coming to terms with his homosexuality while dealing with his alcoholism. He tells of an AA friend who told him: "Your job now is to learn to live with your homosexuality, to make the best of a difficult bargain."

046 B., W. "The Support We All Need." Box 1980 ["The Grapevine"] January 1980: 15-7.

The author comments on what s/he sees as the all too common jokes about homosexuals and other minorities around AA. W.B.'s argument is that "If we are interested in attracting all alcoholics, we need to show them through our words and other behavior that our talk about love and acceptance is something more than talk."

047 Baim, Tracy. "Being Lesbian and Alcoholic." Windy City Times 1.1 (September 26, 1985): 11+.

The article explains basic AA concepts and how they relate to lesbian alcoholics.

048 Bauman, Robert. The Gentleman from Maryland: The Conscious of a Gay Conservative. New York: Arbor House, 1986.

Former Congressman Bauman's homosexuality and alcoholism are the focus of this autobiography.

049 ---. Personal Story. The Courage to Change. Ed. Dennis Wholey. Boston: Houghton, Mifflin, 1984. 147-59.

Bauman presents the story of his alcoholism and

recovery. Special emphasis is placed on his homosexuality and his work as a Member of Congress.

050 Bay, Melissa. "Revolutionary Trails." <u>Plexis</u> 6.6 (1979): 6.

Cartoon which reads in part: "I had this dream that the patriarchy hypnotized the women's community into taking a weird potion that made them get confused & fuzzy & powerless, disconnected from everyone else." The potion was alcohol.

051 <u>Bay Windows</u> 25-30 May 1985.

A special issue devoted to alcoholism which includes: Betty's "The Al-Anon RX," Christine Burton's "Celebrating Sobriety with Amethyst Women," Robert Boucheron's "Frank," Rich Grzesiak's "Truman Capote," Rudy Kikel's "Alcoholism in the Gay and Lesbian Community," Bill Kreidler's "Help is Available for Gay Alcoholics," F.M.'s "A Dyke's Drunkalogue," and Stacy Samson's "Talented, Dry Dykes."

052 Beaton, Stephen and Naome Guild. "Treatment for Gay Problem Drinkers." <u>Social Casework</u> 57 (1976): 302-8.

The article is a case study of a group designed to treat lesbian and gay alcoholics. "The authors believe that the lack of success of many group treatment attempts with gay clients has been due to limiting their emphasis to the problems of being gay [or lesbian] or changing sexual preference, rather than emphasizing the total problems which led clients to request help."

053 Beatty, Roger L. "Alcoholism and the Adult Gay Male Population of Pennsylvania." Thesis. Pennsylvania State University, 1983.

"...various studies and surveys are found to be supportive of an estimate high at-risk incidence for alcoholism among the adult gay male population of Pennsylvania. Recommendations are made concerning this newly identified at-risk population regarding effective and appropriate prevention and treatment of alcoholism."

054 Beaudouard, Jack. *Psychosociologie de L'Homosexualite Masculine*. ris: La Société d'Exploitation de L'Imprimerie Lienhart et Compagnie a Aubenas, 1971.

The book includes a section on alcoholism in the homosexual community.

055 Beckman, L.J. "Self-Esteem of Women Alcoholics." *Journal of Studies on Alcohol* 39 (1978): 491-98.

Twenty percent of the alcoholic women in this study reported at least some homosexual experience. Six percent considered themselves to be homosexual and three percent labeled themselves bi-sexual.

056 Bell, Alan B. and Martin S. Weinberg. *Homosexualities: A Study of Diversity Among Men and Women*. New York: Simon and Schuster, 1978.

Includes material on lesbian and gay bars. The focus, however, is cruising and not alcohol use.

057 Bennett, G., C. Vourakis, and D.S. Woolf, eds. *Substance Abuse: Pharmacologic, Developmental, and Clinical Perspectives*. New York: John Wiley and Sons, 1983.

Includes C. Vourakis' "Homosexuals in Substance Abuse Treatment."

058 Berg, Charles and Clifford Allen. *The Problem of Homosexuality* New York: Citadel, 1958.

Includes Clifford Allen's essay "Homosexuality: Its Nature, Causation, and Treatment.

059 Berg, Stanley E. "Drug Abuse as the Co-Factor in AIDS Deaths: A CDC Cover-up or More CDC Bungling?" Indianapolis: Berg Investment Corporation, 1985.

Distributed as a press release by The Works, Berg suggests that it is a "fluke that AIDS first appeared in the gay population." He claims that "the CDC ignored the almost too obvious link between drug abuse and AIDS deaths."

060 ---. "Drug Abuse as the Co-Factor in AIDS Deaths: A CDC Cover-up or More CDC Bungling?" The Works 5.3 (1985): 24-7+.

A reprint of the press release of the same title.

061 Berg, Steven L. "But I Don't Believe in God: Spirituality and Alcoholism Recovery." Developing a Positive Lesbian/Gay Identity Conference, Detroit, MI, 4 May 1986.

Implications of the spiritual nature of alcoholism recovery programs for lesbians and gay men are discussed. Special emphasis is on AA and Al-Anon.

062 ---. "God as We Understand Him: An Annotated Bibliography." National Association of Lesbian and Gay Alcoholism Professionals' Conference, Chicago, September 1985.

This paper addresses the Christian nature of AA's spirituality and why some lesbians and gay men reject AA because of their discomfort with the Christian spiritual tradition. Reasons for this rejection are given. Many examples are cited from the small press.

063 ---. "Don't Share Needles." Cleveland Gay People's Chronicle 1.7 (1986): 13.

This article is a reprint of of "Substance Abuse and AIDS" distributed by Dignity/Region 5's Substance Abuse Task Force.

064 ---. "Drunks Make Poor Revolutionaries: Alcoholism in the Lesbian/Gay Community." Lesbian/Gay Pride Week, Ann Arbor, MI, 25 June 1986.

Berg focuses on denial by the alcoholic, co-alcoholic, and the homosexual community toward alcoholism. Comparisons between the destructive nature of chemical addiction and AIDS is also made.

065 ---. "Drunks Make Poor Revolutionaries: Alcoholism in the Lesbian and Gay Community." The Agenda 1.6 (1986): 10.

This article is an edited version of Berg's lecture of the same title.

066 ---. "Homosexuality's Challenge to Christianity." College Theology Society. Session on Minorities and the Marginated. Newport, RI, June 1985.

Berg quotes Anne Garrison's "Homily for Integrity/Chicago" in which she finds that societal prejudice, in part, drives homosexuals to alcoholic self-destruction. He finds that because of "acceptance, love, togetherness, and commitment" homosexuals are learning to overcome the self-destructive behavior Garrison identified.

067 ---. Rev. "Alcoholism and Homosexuality." Alcoholism and Human Sexuality. By Gary G. Forrest. NALGAP News 7.3 (1986): 2-3.

Berg is critical of the essay because Forrest virtually ignores the research which has come out in the past 20 years.

068 [---]. "Substance Abuse and AIDS." East Lansing: Dignity/Region 5 Substance Abuse Task Force, [1985].

A review of Alcoholism, Drugs, and AIDS by the San Francisco AIDS/Substance Abuse Task Force and Shooting

Up and Your Health by the Haight-Ashbury Free Medical Clinic.

069 [---]. "Substance Abuse and AIDS." *Cruise Magazine* 7.25 (1985): 14-5.

Reprint of "Substance Abuse and AIDS" distributed by Dignity/Region 5's Substance Abuse Task Force.

070 ---. "Substance Abuse and AIDS." *The Works* 4.11 (1986): 34.

Reprint of "Substance Abuse and AIDS" distributed by Dignity/Region 5's Substance Abuse Task Force.

071 Bergler, Edmund. *The Basic Neurosis: Oral Regression and Psychic Masochism.* 1944. New York: Grune and Stratton, 1977.

Although Bergler found "the coincidence of drinking and homosexuality is possible," he did not conclude that homosexuality caused alcoholism.

072 ---. "Contributions to the Psychogenesis of Alcohol Addiction." *Quarterly Journal of Studies on Alcoholism* 5 (1944): 434-49.

Bergler believes that the only connection between male homosexuality and alcoholism is that both have an oral basis.

073 "A Better Kind of Music." *The Way Back.* 1981. Whitman-Walker Clinic: Washington, DC, 1982. 49-56.

A lesbian musician tells of her period of active alcoholism and how she learned to stay sober in AA.

074 Betty. "The Al-Anon RX: One Day at a Time." *Bay Windows* 25-30 May 1985: 22.

Betty writes: "I went to Al-Anon three months ago to learn how to get my lover to stop drinking and to go to

Alcoholics Anonymous (AA). I learned to change myself instead." The Al-Anon program is then discussed.

075 Bigelow, N.J.T., S.R. Lehrmann, and J.N. Palmer. "Personality in Alcoholic Disorders: Acute Hallucinosis and Delirium Tremens." Psychiatric Quarterly 13 (1939): 732-40.

The authors found that the alcoholic male "shows definite evidence of homoerotism and increased affective response."

076 Bills, Norman. "The Personality Structure of Alcoholics, Homosexuals, and Paranoids as Revealed by Their Responses to the Thematic Apperception Test." Dissertation. Western Reserve University, 1953.

The dissertation includes material on alcoholism.

077 Bissell, LeClair. "The Homosexual AA Member: A Descriptive Study." National Council on Alcoholism Conference, Seattle, May, 1980.

Although several sources mention this paper, it was never compiled and distributed as a formal conference paper.

078 Bittle, William E. "Alcoholics Anonymous and the Gay Alcoholic." Journal of Homosexuality 7.4 (1982): 81-88.

The abstract included with this article reads, in part: "It is proposed that there are a number of characteristics of AA, as it is represented in meetings, which discourage participation by gay people. These characteristics are reviewed, and suggestions are made for providing homosexual alcoholics with support and with the tools for reasonably secure sobriety."

079 Blum, Eva Maria. "Psychoanalytic View of Alcoholism: A Review." Quarterly Journal of Studies on Alcohol 27 (1966): 259-99.

"This article presents a critical review of psychoanalytic theories which deal with the addictions and with alcholism in particular. Includes a section on the theory that alcoholism is caused by latent homosexuality."

080 Blume, Sheila B. "Diagnosis, Casefinding, and Treatment of Alcohol Problems in Women." Alcoholism in Women. Ed. Christen C. Eddy and John L. Ford. Dubuque: Kendall/Hunt Publishing Company, 1980.

Lesbianism is mentioned as one of the subtypes of women alcoholics. "[C]asefinding for the lesbian alcoholic" is mentioned as an "unexplored area."

081 Blumenfeld, Warren. "Alcoholism: The Disease We Can't Ignore." Gay Community News 2 June 1984: 8+.

Using case studies, interviews, and statistical information, Blumenfeld discusses the disease of alcoholism and its affect on the homosexual community. Special emphasis is placed on "Denial," "Effect on Others," "A Way Out," and "Community Support."

082 Boerger, Jeanette. "The Lesbian or Gay Parent: Dependent or Co-Dependent." NALGAP News 6.3 (1985): 5.

Boerger writes that because there are no models for lesbian/gay parents (where chemical addiction is a factor), it is time to begin asking the questions by which models can be formed for dealing with their children.

083 "Book Review." Rev. of The Invisible Alcoholics. By Marian Sandmaier. NAGAP News 1.3 (1980): 6.

A favorable review with special focus on the section of The Invisible Alcoholics which concerns lesbians.

084 "Boston Program Addresses Needs of Gay Alcoholics." NIAAA Information and Feature Service 83 (1981): 2.

Description of the Homophile Alcoholism Treatment Service (HATS).

085 Botwinick, J. and S. Machover. "A Psychometric Examination of Latent Homosexuality in Alcoholism." Quarterly Journal of Studies on Alcohol 12 (1951): 268-72.

The authors state their thesis as "The purpose of the present study is to examine psychometrically the hypothesis that alcoholism expresses, defends against, or in some other way develops as a result of, underlying homosexual motivation." They conclude that "homosexuality cannot be an essential factor in alcoholism, although it may play a dynamic role in individual cases."

086 Boucheron, Robert. "Frank." Bay Windows 25-30 May 1985: 17.

A poem about a gay, recovering alcoholic.

087 Bowman, Karl K. and Morton E. Jellinck. "Alcohol Addiction and Its Treatment." Quarterly Journal of Studies on Alcohol 2 (1941): 98-176.

In part, the authors describe "The most widely known psychoanalytic theory of alcohol addiction is its interpretation in terms of reputed homosexuality." They present the evidence on both sides of the question but offer no conclusion of their own.

088 Bowring, Dick. "Bar Employees Hear Alcohol Abuse." Gay Community News 10 November 1979: 6.

This article is mentioned in The Alternative Press Index.

089 ---. "HATS Helps Alcoholics." Gay Community News 8 December 1979: 10.

The article discusses alcoholism in the gay community and the services offered by the Homophile Alcoholism Treatment Service (HATS) which is in its fifth year of operation.

090 Brady East Sexually Transmitted Disease Clinic. Safer Sex: A Simple Guide for Gay Men Milwaukee: BEST Clinic, 1240 E. Brady, Milwaukee, WI 53202, [nd].

The pamphlet argues that "Alcohol, tobacco, poppers, marijuana, speed, and other recreational drugs wear down your body's overall health."

091 Bromberg, Walter and Paul Schilder. "Psychological Considerations in Alcohol Hallucinations: Castration and Dismembering Motives." International Journal of Psychoanalysis 14 (1933): 206-24.

Among their conclusions, Bromer and Schilder emphasize the homosexual identification of voices during hallucinosis as well as the "anal or homosexual trends in hallucinations of every case of acute alcoholic hallucinosis."

092 Brooks, V.R. Minority Stress and Lesbian Women. Lexington, MA: Lexington Books, 1981.

Brooks notes that: "Throughout the literature of deviancy one finds homosexuality grouped with drug addiction, alcoholism, prostitution, and criminality."

093 Brown, Tim. "The Real Killers." Gay Community News 24 September 1983: 4.

While not discounting the seriousness of AIDS, Brown writes that Christianity, cigarettes, and alcohol are the main killers of lesbians and gay men.

094 Browne-Mayers, A.N., E.E. Seelye, and L. Sillman. "Psychosocial Study of Hospitalized Middle-Class Alcoholic Women." Annals of the New York Academy of Sciences 273 (1976): 593-604.

Three percent of the subjects in this study reported "homosexual conflicts."

095 Bulbul. "Ms. Meg." Cartoon. Off Our Backs 12.8 (1982): 27.

The cartoon shows a group of women protesting for social change. A billboard for Oblivion Vodka is prominent in the background. One woman says to another: "Ever get the feeling somebody wants us poor, ignorant, and drunk!!"

096 Burke, Patricia A. "Bar Use and Alienation Among Lesbian and Heterosexual Women Alcoholics." National Alcoholism Forum, Washington, D.C., April 30, 1982.

"The objective of the present study was to compare the use of bars, drinking patterns, and levels of alienation among four groups of women: 1) lesbian alcoholics; 2) heterosexual women alcoholics; 3) lesbian non-alcoholics; 4) heterosexual women non-alcoholics."

097 ---. "Sexual Orientation, Alienation, and Bar Use in Alcoholic Women." unpublished.

This article was based on her "Bar Use and Alienation Among Lesbian and Heterosexual Alcoholics."

098 Burroughs, William S. Queer. New York: Viking Press, 1985.

Much of the focus in this novel involves the main character's chemical use.

099 Burtle, Vasanti. Women Who Drink: Alcoholic Experience and Psychotherapy. Springfield: Charles C. Thomas, 1979.

The book includes Vernelle Fox's "Clinical Experience in Working with Women With Alcoholism," Dorothy B.

North's "Skid Row Women," and Jessie Potter's "Women and Sex."

100 Burton, Christine. "Celebrating Sobriety with Amethyst Women." Bay Windows 25-30 May 1985: 18.

A description of Boston's Amethyst Women "organized in 1976 to provide an alcohol-free social place for recovering alcoholic lesbians." The group now "offers drug and alcohol-free social events for all women."

101 Buss, Shirley. "Barbara Weathers: From the Bottle to the Barricade." Lesbian Tide 6.2 (1976): 2-3+.

This profile tells Weathers' life as an alcoholic, her recovery, and how she helped establish Los Angeles' Alcohol Center for Women.

102 Button, A.D. "The Psychodynamics of Alcoholism: A Survey of 87 Cases." Quarterly Journal of Studies on Alcohol 17 (1956): 443-60.

Button argues that latent homosexuality is a force in the development of alcoholism if homosexuality "is meant [as] a pattern of incomplete and distorted identifications..."

103 Bychowski, Gustav. "Homosexuality and Psychosis." Perversions: Psychodynamics and Therapy. Ed. Sandor Lorand and Michael Balint. New York: Random House, 1956. 97-130.

Bychowski includes a section where he discusses the relationship of latent homosexuality to alcoholism. His study, unlike most of this time, also discusses lesbians.

104 Cameron, Norman. Personality Development and Psychology: A Dynamic Approach. Boston: Houghton Mifflin, 1963.

Cameron writes that in alcoholics "sex behavior ranged from markedly reduced heterosexual activity to homosexual relations." However, because of "the prevalent view that alcoholism is related to homosexuality," none of the patients in Zwerling's 'Alcoholism Addiction in Personality' was homosexual and only one had more homosexual activity than heterosexual activity."

105 Campbell, Anne [pseud]. "God's Love is Priceless." Lesbian Nuns. Ed. Rosemary Curb and Nancy Manahan. New York: Warner Books, 1986. 213-219.

Campbell tells of her life as a nun, leaving the convent, accepting her lesbianism, and eventually joining AA to get help for her alcoholism.

106 Carey, Greg. "Help for Gays with Alcohol/Drug Problems." The Connection 46 (1984): 1+.

Carey gives an overview of both alcoholism and co-addiction.

107 "Case Histories in Drinking." Unitarian Universalist Lesbian/Gay Word April/May 1983: 3.

A discussion of co-addiction which offers suggestions as to what a family might do if one of the members is an alcoholic. Homosexuality is not specifically mentioned.

108 Catherine. "An Address to Alcoholic Lesbians by a Drunken Dyke." Lesbian Connection 1.5 (1975): 18-20.

Catherine writes "to those of you who are alcoholics and who know you are because you find yourselves attracted to the title of this article in the hopes that you may be able to squeeze from its paragraphs some description of alcoholism which does not apply to you..." Her's is a plea to stop drinking.

109 ---. Letter. Lesbian Connection 1.5 (1975): 17-18.

Catherine takes issue with two points in Kristi's "Lesbians and Alcoholism." First, she believes that viewing alcoholism in stages could lead some women to dismiss their problem. Second, she writes that help does not come from without until it comes from within. She was, however, glad to see the issue of alcoholism being raised.

110 Chapman, Graham. Personal Story. The Courage to Change. By Dennis Wholey. Boston: Houghton Mifflin, 1984. 74-84.

In telling what it was like to stop drinking, Chapman makes the following reference to his homosexuality: "I never hid the fact that I was drinking. I was always very overt about that. I suppose that's from having been truthful and open at age twenty-five about the homosexual part of my life."

111 Chatlos, M. "What If We Were All Clean/Sober?" Lesbian Connection 5 (1984): 18.

This essay is cited in The Alternative Press Index 16.1 (1984): 2.

112 "Chemical Dependency Institute Formed." The Gay News-Telegraph 5.7 (1986): 4.

A description of Pride Institute, the first treatment facility designed around the needs of lesbians and gay men.

113 "Chemical High Life of the '70s: The Ups and Downs of Drug Abuse." Advocate 30 June 1976: 21-7.

This is a special section of drug abuse includes Norman D. Kramer's "The Gay Man's Drug," Randy Shilts' "Alcoholism," Karen West's "Really Down," and Bob Williams' "Downers, Uppers, and Hallucinogens."

114 Chenitz, W.C. and J.M. Swanson, eds. From Grounded Theory to Clinical Practice: Qualitative Research in Nursing. Menlo Park, CA: Addison-Wesley, 1986.

This book includes Robert J. Kus' "From Grounded Theory to Clinical Practice."

115 Christenson, Susan anb Gayle Ihlenfeld. Lesbians, Gay Men, and Their Alcohol and Other Drug Use: Resources. Madison: Wisconsin Clearinghouse for Alcohol and Other Drug Information, 1980.

A good resource list for lesbians and gay men which includes sections on "Alcohol Pamphlets," "Film," "Articles From the Professional Literature," "Awareness Materials," and "National Resources."

116 Christian, Meg. "For the Alcoholism Center for Women, Los Angeles." Frontiers 4.2 (1979): 34.

In this song, Christian discusses her alcoholism and her recovery at the Alcoholism Center for Women.

117 ---. "Turning It Over." Out From Under. Ed. Jean Swallow. Spinsters, Ink, 1983. 50-1.

Words and music to Christian's song of her process of recovery from alcoholism.

118 Cirelli, Dorothy and Tom Rooney. "Treating the Gay and Lesbian Alcoholic." unpublished manuscript.

The authors conclude that for homosexual alcoholics "suffering, treatment and recovery are exactly the same as any alcoholics (with a few variations of perspective)."

119 "City Funded Gay Counselor Tames Alcohol." Advocate 24 April 1974: 20.

News article about Russell Smith who heads the newly

opened Alcoholism Center for Homosexuals in San Francisco.

120 Clark, L.P. "Some Psychological Aspects of Alcoholism." New York Medical Journal 109 (1919): 930-33.

Clark found that alcoholic hallucinations "can be found to be a form of persecution mania arising from unconscious and denied homosexuality." He also argues that "Women who have a strong desire for liquor are likely to prove homosexual."

121 Climent, Carlos E., et al. "Epidemiological Studies of Female Prisoners: Homosexual Behavior." The Journal of Nervous and Mental Disease" 164.1 (1977): 25-9.

The researches found that the incidence of alcoholism was higher among non lesbian prisoners than it was among lesbian prisoners.

122 "Cocaine." NALGAP News 6.2 (1985): 6-7.

Reprinted from an article in ARCircular, "Cocaine" does not specifically discuss homosexuality.

123 Cochran, Mary. "Alcoholism: A Local Perspective." PLGTF Bulletin 3.9 (1981): 11

Cochran concludes: "It is particularly appropriate that lesbian women press for attention to women addicts and to lesbian addicts in particular. If we do not continue to demand satisfactory services for all women, we will only continue to be destroyed by these monsters in our midst."

124 Cohen, Sidney. "Some Speculations About AIDS and Drugs." Drug Abuse and Alcoholism Newsletter 14.9 (1985).

The author found that drugs, including alcohol, are used by at least 80% of homosexual men with AIDS.

125 Colcher, Ronnie W. "Counseling the Homosexual Alcoholic." Journal of Homosexuality 7.4 (1982): 43-52.

The abstract included with the article reads: "The author summarizes her clinical experience with 75 homosexual alcoholics, 47 male and 28 female, of diverse backgrounds. Similarities of recommendations for the counselor working with homosexual alcoholics is included."

126 Coleman, Eli. "Developmental Stages of the Coming Out Process." Journal of Homosexuality 7.2/3 (1982): 31-43.

Coleman writes that "One common stumbling block to completing the tasks of the exploration stage [of coming out] is the use of intoxicating agents to anesthetize pain or to shore up a weak self-concept." Alcohol and drugs can also be used to cope with emotional pain or they may become associated with sexual expression leading to problems of intimacy.

127 Committee on Substance Abuse and AIDS. Alcohol Drugs and AIDS. San Francisco: San Francisco AIDS Foundation, 1985.

A good explanation of the relationship between alcohol, drugs, and AIDS written in both English and Spanish. The gay community is mentioned under the discussion of poppers.

128 Comité de Abuse de Substancias/AIDS. Alcohol Drogas y AIDS. San Francisco: San Francisco AIDS Foundation, 1985.

Lucrecia Bermúdez's translation of the Committee on Substance Abuse and AIDS' Alcohol Drugs and AIDS. Printed in Spanish and English.

129 Conlin, David and Jamie Smith. "Group Psychotherapy

for Gay Men." Journal of Homosexuality 7.2/3 (1984): 105-12.

Conlin and Smith include a case study of Mr. B., a gay man who had difficulty with prescription medications. As he began to cut down his use of medications, his alcohol intake increased.

130 Connor, S. "New Study Ties Poppers, AIDS." Gay Community News 12 October 1985: 1.

A summary of the findings of a study done at the National Jewish Center for Immunology and Respiratory Medicine that linked poppers and AIDS.

131 Cook, David. "Alcoholism and Gay Men: A Review of the Literature." Rutgers University School of Social Work. Spring, 1980.

A good overview of the literature which is now dated.

132 Corrigan, Eileen M. Alcoholic Women in Treatment. New York: Oxford University Press, 1980.

Six percent of the women who participated in Corrigan's study were lesbians.

133 "Could You Have Written This?" GAZE 3.8 (August 1982): 4.

Article written by a homosexual alcoholic.

134 Covington, Stephanie. "Sex and Violence--The Unmentionables in Alcoholism Treatment." National Alcoholism Forum, Washington, D.C., April 5, 1982.

An overview of Covington's findings for her dissertation, "Sexual Experience, Dysfunction, and Abuse." Some of Covington's subjects were lesbians.

135 ---. "Sexual Experience, Dysfunction, and Abuse: A

Comparative Study of Alcoholic and Non-Alcoholic Women." Dissertation. Union Graduate School, 1982.

Of the 35 middle-class alcoholics studied, 17% described themselves as homosexual and an additional 17% reported a bisexual preference.

136 Cowan, Beth H. "Birth Defects Linked to Maternal Alcoholism." Herself 3.1 (1974): 4.

Brief summary of report "that the data are sufficient to establish that maternal alcoholism can cause abnormal fetal development." Does not address lesbianism specifically.

137 Cox, Kevin M. Rev. of Lesbians, Gay Men, and Their Alcohol and Other Drug Use: Resources. By Susan Christenson and Gayle Ihlenfeld. RFD 28 (1981): 47.

"Christensen and Ihlenfeld have successfully corrected the invisibility of lesbians in treatment literature by selecting a majority of resources with a lesbian or co-sexual focus. And the authors have wisely reminded counselors that clients are seeking help to change their substance dependency--not their sexual preference."

138 Creative Sex, Creative Medicine." New York Native 42.

Tom Smith's letter to the New York Native was written in response to this article.

139 Crémieux, Albert, J. Cain, and J. Rabattu. "Toxicomanie Alcoolique et Orté chez un Déséquilibré de la Sexualité." [Alcohol and Ortedrine Addiction in a Sexual Deviant] Annales Médico-Psychologiques 106 (1948): 497-501.

The title is self explanatory.

140 Crawford, William. Homosexuality in Canada. Toronto: Canadian Gay Archives, 1984.

The bibliography includes a section on alcoholism.

141 Curb, Rosemary and Nancy Manahan, eds. Lesbian Nuns: Breaking the Silence 1985. New York: Warner Books, 1986.

Originally published by Naiad Press, this book includes Anne Campbell's "God's Love is Priceless."

142 Curran, F.J. "Personality Studies in Alcoholic Women." Journal of Nervous and Medical Disease 86 (1937): 645-67.

Four percent of Curran's subjects reported that they had had at least some overt homosexual experience.

143 D., M. "The Happy Hooker." Box 1980 ["The Grapevine"] 42.7 (1985): 8-9.

The author says that he never hoped to be "a liar, thief, cheat, gay person, nut, drug addict, jailbird, or alcoholic, but somehow I managed to make it in all those categories." Homosexuality not mentioned again in his article.

144 Daniel. "Change: The Key Word." RFD 12.4 (1986): 25.

In this discussion of AIDS, Daniel writes that "There are so many abuses that we can participate in that will damage or shut down the immune system--i.e. drugs, excessive sex, prolonged depression..."

145 [David.] "Case History: David." Unitarian Universalist Lesbian/Gay Word April/May 1983: 7.

A brief paragraph which tells of David's involvement in (gay) AA.

146 Dean, Dawson F. "Significant Characteristics of the Homosexual Personality." Dissertation. New York University, 1938.

Alcoholism is discussed in the dissertation.

147 Dean, R.B. and H. Richardson. "Analysis of MMPI Profiles of 40 College Educated Homosexuals." Journal of Consulting Psychology 28 (1964): 483-86.

This article is cited in Gary MacPherson's "The Homosexual Homophobia of the Gay Alcoholic as a Factor for Consideration in the Treatment of Alcoholism."

148 De Larson. Rev. of Out From Under. By Jean Swallow. Soujourner: The Women's Forum (February 1984): 16.

Favorably impressed with the book, De Larson writes: "I'm hoping that this book will help lesbians to re-examine their drug and alcohol use, and to make important decisions that will affect their own lives and those of every lesbian in our community."

149 de Monteflores, Carmen and Stephen J. Schultz. "Coming Out: Similarities and Differences for Lesbians and Gay Men." Journal of Social Issues 34.3 (1978): 59-73.

The authors make reference to the "boy-was-I-drunk syndrome" as one way gay men deny their feelings or actions.

150 De Soto, Lisa. "If I Should Die Before I Wake." Lesbian Tide 9.5 (1980): 8-9.

De Soto tells her story of what it was like, what happened, and what it is like today. She discusses the support she found in Los Angeles' Alcoholism Center for Women, Women for Sobriety, Alcoholics Together, and a group called Alternatives to AA. She concludes: "I am fortunate that I am sober today, after many years of struggling, to share my experience with you. Many of my sisters are not. Some have died, others are still feeling the slow decay I once knew."

151 De Stefano, George. "Gay Drug Abuse: Owning Up to a Serious Problem." Advocate 24 June 1986: 42-7.

A general explanation of the problem of alcohol and drug abuse in the lesbian/gay community.

152 ---. "Drug Abuse and AIDS: Troubling Connections." Advocate 24 June 1986: 47.

The article focuses on the work of Cesar Caceres, an expert in medical statistics who has questioned the method which the Center for Disease Control uses in reporting AIDS statistics. Material which suggests that drug abuse is linked to unsafe sex techniques is also presented.

153 Deborah. "Amethyst Women...Socializing..." Gay Community News 15 July 1978: 11.

This article is cited in The Alternative Press Index 10.3 (1970): 2.

154 Degan, Kathleen and Joan Waitkevicz. "Lesbian Health Issues." British Journal of Sexual Medicine (May 1982).

The authors "describe health problems of lesbians in five areas: sexually transmitted diseases, alcoholism, mental health, sexual dysfunction, as victims of incest and some general medical information. An interview technique for primary care physicians is suggested.

155 Delphos. Gay Men and Lesbian Women in Treatment Key West: Florida Keys Memorial Hospital, [nd].

Pamphlet describing services available to the homosexual community at Delphos, the Alcohol and Drug Treatment Center at Florida Keys Memorial Hospital, 5900 W. Jr. College Road, Key West, FL 33040.

156 "Dear Angry." Rising Up Angry 16 July 1972: 7.

The author's thesis is that: "Because of the day to day struggle trying to make it in this society people need crutches like this [alcohol and heroin] and the pig capitalists are more than willing to put another control on our lives as long as they make a buck." The author claims that practicing alcoholics care only for their liquor. But those who get help begin to care about their brothers and sisters.

157 D'Eramo, James E. "Poppers: The Writing on the Wall." *New York Native* 14-17 June 1984: 9.

D'Eramo implicates nitrite inhalants as a co-factor in AIDS.

158 Diamond, Deborah L. and Sharon S. Wilsnack. "Alcohol Abuse Among Lesbians: A Descriptive Study." *Journal of Homosexuality* 4.2 (1978): 123-42.

The abstract included with the text reads: "Intensive interviews with 10 lesbian alcohol abusers revealed strong dependency needs, low self esteem, and a high incidence of depression....The findings suggest that lesbians with alcohol problems need (a) therapists who will accept their sexual orientation and (b) treatment that will help them increase their sense of power and self-esteem without alcohol."

159 Diehl, Edward M. "Treatment for Lesbians and Gay Men. What to Look For." *PLGTF Bulletin* 3.9 (1981): 10.

Diehl discusses treatment facilities in terms of the homosexual client. He concludes that one of "the major obstacles alcoholic lesbians and gay men face when contemplating treatment are the barriers we place before ourselves."

160 Dietrich, Donna. "Reaching Out to the Lesbian Alcoholic." National Alcoholism Forum, Seattle, 3 May 1980.

The paper tells how McCambridge House in Springfield, Illinois tried to attract lesbian alcoholics.

161 DJ. "What the Family Can Do to Help." Unitarian Universalists Lesbian/Gay Word (April/May 1983): 4.

DJ is a 35 year old mother of three, now married to her lesbian lover of four years. This is her story of addiction and recovery.

162 Do You Think You're Different? New York: Alcoholics Anonymous, 1976.

The purpose of the pamphlet is to demonstrate the diversity of individuals who are involved in AA. It includes Padric's "My Name is Padric and I'm an Alcoholic (gay)" and Mary's "My Name is Mary and I'm an Alcoholic (lesbian)."

163 Doe, Johnny. [pseud] Interview. The Homosexuals. By Alan Ebert. New York: Macmillan, 1977. 240 59.

In this interview, Doe discusses his alcoholism and recovery. "Issues around reaction to gay clients in non-gay treatment agencies, accessibility of services, and survey problems in the gay community are discussed with their implications for improving services like HATS [Homophile Alcohol Treatment Service]."

164 Dombrowski, Mark. "Alcohol Use and Abuse in Gay Literature." NALGAP Mid-West Regional Conference, East Lansing, MI, 11 April 1986.

Dombrowski demonstrates how alcohol and sex are linked in most gay literature. Due to the educational nature of literature, the role models presented in most books give poor models for living soberly.

165 "Drinking Myths: A Guided Tour Through Folklore, Fantasy, Humbug, and Hogwash." Unitarian Universalist Lesbian/Gay Word (April/May 1983): 5.

A list of myths about alcohol and alcoholism. Homosexuality is not specifically mentioned.

166 Driscoll, R. "A Gay Identified Alcohol Treatment Program: A Follow-up Study." Journal of Homosexuality 7 (1982): 71-80.

A discussion of HATS, the Homophile Alcohol Treatment Service, an urban Boston out-patient treatment clinic.

167 Durack, David T. "Opportunistic Infections and Kaposi's Sarcoma in Homosexual Men." New England Journal of Medicine (10 December 1981).

In this editorial, Durak writes that "Some new factor may have distorted the host-parasite relation." Recreational drugs are a distinct possibility.

168 [Dyke, Jennifer]. "On Behalf of a Minority." Alcohol Education and Training News 2.6 (1979): 4-5.

A general discussion of issues related to treating homosexual alcoholics.

169 "Eagleville Conference Examines Ethical Issues in Treatment." NIAAA Information and Feature Service 65 (1979): 2.

Thomas O. Ziebold's comments that: "Sexual minorities...cannot simply be put through the treatment 'mill'" are examined.

170 East, W. Norwood. "Sexual Offenders." Journal of Nervous and Mental Disease 103 (1946): 626-66.

East, in mentioning the theory that alcoholism is caused by latent homosexuality, concludes, however, that "many [alcoholics] are strongly heterosexual and personal experience leaves me in no doubt that more heterosexual than homosexual crimes are due to alcohol."

171 Ebert, Alan. The Homosexuals. New York: Macmillan, 1977.

The book includes Johnny Doe's "Interview."

172 Eddy, C.C. and J.L. Ford, eds. Alcoholism in Women. Dubuque, IA: Kendall/Hunt, 1980.

The book includes Brenda Weathers' "Alcoholism and the Lesbian Community."

173 Ellis, Don. "Alcoholism on the Gay Scene." QQ (July/August 1979): 21-2+.

Ellis discusses the role of the bar in the gay community from both an historic and contemporary perspective. The role of alcohol in the bars is presented giving special emphasis to the ways in which alcohol inhibits cruising and sexual activity.

174 Ernst, R.S. and P.S. Houts. "Characteristics of Gay Persons with Sexually Transmitted Diseases." Sexually Transmitted Diseases 12.2 (1985): 59-63.

Among gay men, gonorrhea and syphilis were associated, in part, with high scores on the Brief Michigan Alcohol Screening Test. For lesbians, the correlation was with heterosexual activity.

175 Estes, Nada J. and M. Edith Heinemann, eds. Alcoholism: Development, Consequences, and Interventions. St. Louis: C.V. Mosby, 1982.

The book includes Edith S. Gomberg's "Women with Alcohol Problems."

176 Evans, Sue and Sue Shaefer. "Why Women's Sexuality is Important to Address in Chemical Dependency Programs." Grassroots (September 1980).

The authors write that "Many women who have not dealt with their sexuality in prior treatments report that they returned to drinking/drugs in order to protect themselves from painful feelings surrounding their sexuality in areas such as prostitution, sexual preference, incest, abortion, fear of sex sober, having indiscriminate sex, or in being preorgasmic." Assistance given lesbians at Chrysalis Treatment Center is mentioned.

177 Eve, Sharon I. "A Comprehensive Alcoholism Prevention Program: Integration of Individual Services and Community Oriented Approaches." Los Angeles: Alcoholism Center for Women, nd.

Lesbians are listed as a high risk category for alcoholism.

178 F., Ron. "We Met That Evening and He Told Me All About Himself and How He Had Stayed Sober..." RFD 28 (1981): 36.

Ron offers a brief account of his alcoholism and of his recovery through AA. Of special interest is his discussion of Fred, his lover of 23 years and the fact that they are "rural" gay men.

179 "Fact Sheet on Women and Alcoholism." Los Angeles: Alcoholism Center for Women, nd.

A list of facts about how alcohol affects women.

180 Fain, Nathan. "Is It Safe to Sniff?: The Controversy Over Poppers and Other Inhalant Drugs." Advocate 5 August 1982: 23-5+.

A general overview of the effects of various inhalants.

181 Faith. "Four." Out From Under. Ed. Jean Swallow. San Francisco: Spinsters, Ink, 1983. 27-33.

Faith writes that: "More than six years ago, a wild eyed, shaking, desperate failure walked into a room full of strangers and began a metamorphosis that is still in its initial stages." This essay addresses four stages of her change: revolution, absolution, persecution, and evolution.

182 "Fantasy vs. Intimacy." NALGAP News 6.1 (1984): 8.

The article describes a workshop developed by Bill Knudtson which helps gay men learn more about intimacy.

183 Feller, Deborah. "Crack in the Door." NALGAP News 7.4 (1986): 5.

In her article, Feller places the problem with Crack in the broader perspective of chemical addiction.

184 Fenichel, O. The Psychoanalytic Theory of Neurosis. New York: W.W. Norton, 1945.

Homosexuality is cited as a cause of alcoholism.

185 Fenwick, R.D. The Advocate Guide to Gay Health. 1978. Alyson: Boston, 1982.

The chapter on "Alcoholism and Other Drugs" includes physiological information as well as material on alcoholism and co-alcoholism. Also, in "The Hazards of Sex," Fenwick emphasizes that most of the hazards result from substance abuse.

186 Fettner, Ann Giudici. "Bringing Scientists to Their Senses: Cesar Caceres vs. Selective Blindness." Christopher Street 9.3 (1985): 15-8.

The article focuses on the studies of Cesar Caceres an expert in medical statitics who "maintains that 79% of those with AIDS in this country should be categorized as drug abusers." The selective blindness behind the Center for Disease Control's refusal to investigate the AIDS/drug abuse link is emphasized.

187 Fifield, Lilene, et al. "Alcoholism and the Gay Community." unpublished manuscript.

A 32 page summary of "On My Way Nowhere."

188 ---. "Key Note Speech." National Alcoholism Forum, Seattle, 3 May 1980.

A good overview of issues related to alcoholism in the homosexual community.

189 ---. "On My Way Nowhere: Alienated, Isolated, and Drunk--An Analysis of Gay Alcohol Abuse and an Evaluation of Alcoholism Rehabilitation Services for the Los Angeles Gay Community." 1975.

A statistical study of the drinking patterns of homosexual men and men in the Los Angeles area and a survey of gay and non-gay treatment facilities. Currently, this is the study cited as the statistical authority on alcoholism and the gay community.

190 "5th Anniversary for Gay/Lesbian Newtown Alano Club." Gaylife (August 29, 1985).

The article describes the services offered at the Newtown Alano Club.

191 Finnegan, Dana G. "Testimony: New York City Task Force on Women and Alcoholism." New York City, 17 February 1981.

Finnegan offers recommendations on how better to provide services for the lesbian alcoholic.

192 ---. "Written Testimony Presented to the Members of the Committee on National Strategies for AIDS." 17 May 1986.

Finnegan focuses on the link between AIDS and chemical addiction. Because agencies and groups which are working with persons with AIDS and the "worried well" often are not well versed in chemical dependency, gay men are often the victims of homophobia and alcoholaphobia.

193 Finnegan, Dana G. and David Cook. "Special Issues Affecting the Treatment of [Gay] Male and Lesbian Alcoholics." Alcoholism and Sexual Dysfunction. Ed. David J. Powell. New York: Haworth Press, 1984. 85-98.

Finnegan and Cook argue that "In order to treat their gay and lesbian clients in constructive and health-enhancing ways, counselors must be able to determine when to focus on their client's alcoholism and basically ignore their sexual orientation and when to attend closely to client's sexual orientation and the interplay between it and the alcoholism."

194 Finnegan, Dana G. and Ed Ellis. "Lesbians and Gay Males: Adult Children of Alcoholism." 10% of Those We Serve Conference, New York, NY, 26 February 1986.

The paper outlines the parallels between the experience of adult children of alcoholics and the gay man or lesbian.

195 Finnegan, Dana G., Emily McNally, and Glen Fisher. "Alcoholism and Chemical Dependency." Sourcebook on Lesbian/Gay Issues. Ed. F. Schwaber and M. Shernoff. New York: National Gay Health Education Foundation, 1984. 47-9.

A strong overview of factors which contribute to alcohol/drug abuse in the homosexual community.

196 Finnegan, Dana G. and Emily McNally. "Alcoholism, Recovery, and Health: Lesbian and Gay Men." National Council on Alcoholism Forum, Seattle, May, 1980.

The paper "describe[s] and discuss[es] the process of un-learning and re-learning that alcoholism professionals need to engage in if they wish to deliver high quality treatment to the recovering gay/lesbian alcoholic."

197 ---. Dual Identities: Counseling Chemically Dependent Gay Men and Lesbians. Center City, MN: Hazelden, 1987.

This book focuses on the special issues that people struggling with chemical dependency and homophobia must face and work through in order to recovery. It examines the processes by which people come to terms with the stigmatized identities of being chemically dependent and homosexual. The book discusses the skills that counselors need in order to be helpful to their clients. In addition, the book includes resources, suggested readings, and an organizational audit for evaluating a program's sensitivity to lesbian/gay issues.

198 [---]. Editorial. NAGAP News 2.3 (1981): 1.

The authors provide a summary of what the National Association of Gay Alcoholism Professionals accomplished during its first two years.

199 ---. "The First Ever National NALGAP Conference!" NALGAP News 7.1 (1985): 2.

The co-founders of the National Association of Lesbian and Gay Alcoholism Professionals share their reaction to the first national conference sponsored by the organization.

200 ---. "How to See (and Help) the Invisible Lesbian Alcoholic." National Alcohol and Drug Problems of North America Conference, Washington, D.C., August, 1980

Finnegan and McNally discuss why lesbian alcoholics are invisible and why invisibility is a problem. They then offer suggestions as to what can be done to address the problem of invisibility.

201 ---. "Issues Special to Lesbian Alcoholics." _Lesbian and Gay Health_ 1.2 (1984): 13-4.

Using the example of "Jane L.," a lesbian alcoholic, Finnegan and McNally summarize the main points in their "How to See (and Help) the Invisible Lesbian Alcoholic."

202 Finnegan, Dana, Emily McNally, and Tom Smith. "Gay Alcoholism and Substance Abuse: Issues for S[exually] T[ransmitted] D[isease] Workers." _The Official Newsletter of the National Coalition of Gay STD Services_ 5.3 (1984): 17-8.

Guidelines are designed to help lesbian and gay health workers identify and refer people with substance abuse problems to appropriate agencies/support groups for help in overcoming their addiction.

203 "The First National Conference and That's How It Was--September 1985." _NALGAP News_ 7.1 (1985): 1-2.

A general overview of the first national conference of the National Association of Lesbian and Gay Alcoholism Professionals.

204 "Five Year County Plan for the City and County of San Francisco Concerning Lesbian and Gay Male Alcoholism Services and Prevention." June, 1985.

The title is self explanatory.

205 Foote, Travis. "Alcoholism and the Lesbian Community." 373-77.

In this brief article, Foote gives a general description of alcoholism in the lesbian community. Although we have been able to obtain a photo-copy of this article, we have been unable to locate the source. As a result, no further bibliograph information is available.

206 Forrest, Gary G. Alcoholism and Human Sexuality. Springfield: Charles C. Thomas, 1983.

In his chapter on "Alcoholism and Homosexuality," Forrest assumes that homosexuality is a dysfunction which is curable. Most research cited is pre-1965.

207 ---. Alcoholism, Narcissism and Psychopathology. Holmes Beach, FL: Learning Publications, 1982.

Homosexuality as a factor in the development of alcoholism is mentioned throughout the book.

208 ---. Intensive Psychotherapy of Alcoholism. Springfield, IL: Charles C. Thomas, 1984.

Although the "identity and sexually determined paranoid trends of the alcoholic can be related to bisexual and homosexual conflicts," Forrest found that few alcoholics are "explicitly homosexual."

209 Fox, Vernelle. "Clinical Experience in Working with Women with Alcoholism." Women Who Drink. Ed. Vasanti Burtle. Springfield: Charles C. Thomas, 1979. 81-97.

In discussing the groups at the Georgia Clinic in Atlanta, Fox writes: "Issues of age, socioeconomic status, race and sexual preference came up regularly. The feelings surrounding these issues were usually curiosity and awkwardness about surfacing subjects."

210 ---. "The Gay Alcoholic." The University of Utah School on Alcoholism, Salt Lake City, UT, 18-21 June 1979.

Fox maintains that "it is the responsibility of treatment programs to recognize that it has gay clients and to treat their alcoholism adequately." The agency is not responsible "to try to alter their [client's] lifestyle except as it relates to drinking."

211 Francis, R.J., T. Wikstrom, and V. Alcena. "Contracting AIDS as a Means of Committing Suicide." *American Journal of Psychiatry* 142.5 (1985): 656.

Case study of a gay alcoholic with anxiety disorders and suicidal thoughts who sought out persons with AIDS as sex partners.

212 Frank, M. "Three Films About Women, Drugs, and Alcohol." Rev. of *The Last To Know*, *We all Have Our Reasons*, and *Women, Drugs, and Alcohol*. *Off Our Backs* 13.2 (1983): 23.

Brief summary of the three films.

213 Freedman, Mark. "Being Naturally High Much Better." *Advocate* 10 April 1974: 43.

Freedman states that "It is obvious that alcoholism is a complicated, controversial issue. New approaches to drinking problems are emerging. I think that we must explore all of them in order to deal with what is one of the most serious problems in the gay world and in American society." He places emphasis on the social-learning approach.

214 Freudenberger, Herbert J. "The Gay Addict in a Drug and Alcohol Abuse Therapeutic Community." *Homosexual Counseling Journal* 3.1 (1976): 34-45.

Freudenberger writes that "It is a sad but almost invariably true, that to be a gay resident of a therapeutic community leaves the addict open to discrimination, verbal assault and special negative treatment." He outlines some problems homosexuals face in treatment programs and then offers suggestions on how to improve the therapeutic community.

215 ---. "The Therapeutic Community Revisited." *American Journal of Drug and Alcohol Abuse* 3.1 (1976): 33-43.

Freudenberger writes: "Homosexuals need to be given the opportunity to come out. Gays are still too much closeted in programs, often the victims of jokes, derision, and confusion."

216 Friedman-Kein, Alvin E, et al. "Disseminated Kaposi's Sarcoma in Homosexual Men." Annals of Internal Medicine (June 1982): 693-700.

All 19 men in this study used amyl or butyl nitrite inhalants.

217 Fuller, Robert W. "Assessment of Sexual Functioning." Alcoholism and Sexual Dysfunction. Ed. David J. Powell. New York: Hayworth Press, 1985. 49-64.

In discussing how to take a sexual history, Fuller assumes that homosexuality is a sexual problem. He cautions that a clinician must determine "the degree and complexity of the pathology" in working with homosexuals and bi-sexuals.

218 G., F. "Thirsty for Life." Box 1980 ["The Grapevine"] 43.2 (1986): 34-5.

In F.G.'s story, she tells how she was drinking alcoholically even before entering a gay bar.

219 Gangadharam, P.R.J., et al. "Immunosuppressive Action of Isobutyl Nitrite." International Congress on Immunopharmacology, Florence, Italy, May 1985.

In their tests on mice, the researchers demonstrated that nitrite inhalants greatly increased the risk of acquiring AIDS. They conclude that "inhaling isobutyl nitrite should be considered dangerous to homosexuals and others at high risk for developing AIDS."

220 Garrison, Anne C. "Homily for Integrity/Chicago on the Feast of the Holy Innocents." Integrity Forum 8.2 (1982): 21.

Garrison writes that "In its own way, society slaughters the innocent [homosexuals] every day, driving to suicide, alcoholic self-destruction or psychic catatonia those whom it no longer, in these enlightened times, burns at the stake."

221 Gay, George R., et al. "Love and Haight: The Sensuous Hippie Revisited: Drug/Sex Practices in San Francisco, 1980-81." Journal of Psychoative Drugs 14 (1982): 111-23.

This article is cited in: Parker, William. Homosexuality Bibliography: Second Supplement, 1976-1982 Metuchen, NJ: Scarecrow Press, 1985.

222 "Gay AAs No Longer Anonymous." Advocate 17 July 1974: 16.

A news article reporting that AA's General Service Conference had decided to list lesbian/gay AA groups in its directory.

223 "Gay Alcoholics." Alcohol Education and Training News [State of Florida] 2.6 (1979): 1-4.

This general article addresses such issues as "Background Information," "Treatment Problems," "Treatment Resources," and "The Co-Alcoholic."

224 "Gay Alcoholics Targeted at NCA Forum." NIAAA/IFS Special Report: NCA Conference 3 September 1980: 5.

The focus is on Lilene Fifield's research.

225 "Gay Family Systems Seen as Treatment Factor." NIAAA Information and Feature Service 30 June 1981: 7.

The article summarizes Peter N. Nardi's work with same-sex couples and homosexual family systems.

226 "Gay Honesty Needs a Gay Ear." Advocate 27 February 1974: 13.

A general discussion of gay groups being formed within Alcoholics Anonymous.

227 Gay? Lesbian? Alcoholic? East Lansing: Monday Night AA Group, n.d.

A three-fold pamphlet which answers such questions as "Is homosexuality to cause alcoholism?", "Are the gay groups of AA in conflict with the principle that AA does not wish to engage in any controversy?" "What can homosexual alcoholics use to replace liquor?" and "Does a gay alcoholic have a special problem?" The material is taken from the pamphlet Lesbian or Gay and Alcoholic?

228 "Gay/Lesbian Bars: Support System Replaces Family." The U.S. Journal of Drug and Alcohol Dependence 9.11 (1985): 22.

Based on an interview with Robert Kajan, the article focuses on how homosexuals "turn to gay bars to 'develop para-family relationships and a network of emotional closeness.'" Gay/lesbian Alano clubs can serve a similar function.

229 "Gay Male Alcoholism Prevention." PLGTF Bulliten 3.9 (1981): 18.

A description of "Getting High Without Drugs Workshop" series developed by Tom Smith, Dick Dobbins, Eric Olsen, Scott Whitney, Kelly McCoy, and Jim Maddocks. No specific references in article refer to homosexuals.

230 Gay or Lesbian and Alcoholic? New York: International Advisory Council for Homosexual Men and Women in Alcoholics Anonymous, nd.

See Lesbian or Gay and Alcoholic?

231 "Gay Papers Presented to Alcoholism Forum." Seattle Gay News 9 May 1980: 5.

A discussion of the papers presented at the "Alcoholism and the Gay Community Forum" of the National Council on Alcoholism Conference held in Seattle, May 1980.

232 "Gay, Proud, and Sober." Film Review. Journal 8.8 (1979): 12.

The article is mentioned in Wiliam Crawford's Homosexuality in Canada.

233 "Gays and Chemical Dependence." The Gay News-Telegraph 5.7 (1986): 15.

A brief discussion of alcoholism in the gay community citing some of the specific problems sexuality plays in recovery.

234 "Gays on the Wagon." Human Behavior 6.1 (1977): 44.

The article summarizes the findings in Stephen Beaton and Naome Guild's "Treatment for Gay Problem Drinkers."

235 Gibbins, R.J. and R.H. Walters. "Three Preliminary Studies of a Psychoanalytic Theory of Alcohol Addiction." Quarterly Journal of Studies on Alcohol 21 (1960): 618-41.

Gibbins and Walters report on three preliminary investigations performed to study the psychoanalytic theory that links homosexuality to alcoholism. They conclude that "While the experiments as a whole do not provide strong evidence for the psychoanalytic theory, the results suggest that this theory should not be lightly discarded."

236 GLAODA [Gay/Lesbian Alcohol and Other Drug Abuse]. Alcoholism, Drug Abuse, Co-Alcoholism In Our Lesbian and Gay Community: There Are Solutions! Madison: GLAODA, 1981.

Printed for the Second Annual Gay and Lesbian Health Forum, this booklet includes a discussion of the problem and resources available for both alcoholics and co-alcoholics.

237 Goedert, James J., et al. "Amyl Nitrite May Alter T Lymphocytes in Homosexual Men." The Lancet 20 February 1982: 412-16.

In this study of two men with Kaposi's Sarcoma and 15 healthy homosexual volunteers, immunological abnormalities were found in all the the nitrite users, but in only one of the non-users.

238 Gomberg, Edith S. "Problems with Alcohol and Other Drugs." Gender and Disorder. Eds. Edith Gomberg and Violet Franks. New York: Brunner/Mazel, 1979.

Gomberg writes that, with the exception of Lesbian groups, drinking groups which include women are almost invariably composed of men and women and not solely women.

239 ---. "Women with Alcohol Problems." Alcoholism: Development, Consequences, and Interventions. Ed. Nada J. Estes and M. Edith Heineman. St. Louis: C.V. Mosby, 1982. 217-30.

Gomberg notes that homosexual women have a higher degree and different consequences from alcoholism than do heterosexual women. "The consequences for the lesbian women might be called masculine and suggest that a masculine life-style leads to masculine consequences of alcoholism."

240 Gomberg, Edith and Violet Franks, eds. Gender and Disordered Behavior: Sex Differences in Psychopathology. New York: Brunner/Mazel, 1979.

The book includes Bernard F. Riess and Jeanne M. Sfaer's "Homosexuality in Females and Males" and Edith Gomberg's "Problems with Alcohol and Other Drugs."

241 Gonsioreck, John C. Homosexuality and Psychotherapy. New York: Haworth Press, 1982.

Special issue of the Journal of Homosexuality which includes Craig Anderson's "Males as Sexual Assault Victims," Bronwyn Anthony's "Lesbian Client-Lesbian Therapist," David Conlin's "Group Psychotherapy for Gay Men," and Eli Coleman's "The Developmental Stages of the Coming Out Process."

242 Gonzales, R.M. "Hallucinogenic Dependency During Adolescence as a Defense Against Homosexual Fantasies." Journal of Youth and Adolescence 8 (1979): 63-71.

A case study of a 15 year old who used drugs to suppress his homosexual interests.

243 Goode, Eric and Richard R. Troiden. "Amyl Nitrite Use Among Homosexual Men." American Journal of Psychiatry 136.8 (1979): 1067-69.

The authors interviewed 150 homosexual men to determine the relationship between use of amyl nitrite and certain aspects of homosexuality. They found that the use of amyl nitrite is strongly related to a number of unconventional, deviant sexual practices and to certain medically related problems."

244 Goodstein, D.B. "D.B.G." Advocate 25 June 1985: 6.

In writing that gay bar culture dominates everything in the gay community, Goodstein briefly comments on the high rate of alcoholism in the homosexual community.

245 ---. "Opening Space." Advocate 25 February 1974: 5.

The column introduces Randy Shilt's "Alcoholism." Goodstein comments on the need to have non-alcoholic beverages available at gay bars and functions. Robert I. McQueen's "Editorial" on alcoholism appears in the same issue.

246 ---. "Opening Space." Advocate 11 December 1980: 3.

Goodstein writes that "The two greatest enemies of gays are the closet and drug abuse--including alcoholism."

247 Goodwin, Mimi. "Breaking the Silences: Incest and Substance Abuse." First International Lesbian/Gay Health Conference, [Sixth National Lesbian/Gay Health Conference], New York City, 16-19 June 1984.

The paper includes a section which addresses considerations in dealing with lesbian/gay survivors of childhood sexual assault.

248 Graham, L. "Lesbians" 1977-1978 County Plan (Report prepared for San Francisco Department of Public Health), San Francisco.

The report is cited in C. Vourakis' "Homosexuals in Substance Abuse Treatment."

249 Greenberg, J. "A Study of Male Homosexuals (Predominantly College Students)." Journal of the American College Health Association 22.1 (1973): 56-60.

Greenberg found that the incidence of illicit drug use was higher among his homosexual sample than among his control group.

250 Greenblatt, Milton and Mark A, Schuckit. Alcoholism Problems in Women and Children. New York: Grune and Stratton, 1976.

The book includes James L. Hawkin's "Lesbianism and Alcoholism."

251 Greer, Pat. "Finding Our Own Strength." Big Mama Rag 7.11 (1979): 10.

Greer discusses the frustration of watching women kill themselves with alcohol and other drugs.

252 Gruen, A. "Lesbian AA." Gaysweek 31 October 1977: 22.

The article is cited in The Alternative Press Index 9.4 (1977): 2.

253 Grobel, Lawrence. Conversations with Capote. New York: New American Library, 1985.

The book mentions both Capote's alcoholism and homosexuality.

254 Grooms, L. Allen, Jr. "AIDS: Concerns of a Substance Abuse Agency." National Academy of Sciences and the Institute of Medicine, 15 May 1986.

The paper mentions Tom Smith's "AIDS and Substance Abuse Counseling with Gay Men" in a general discussion of AIDS and substance abuse counseling.

255 Grzesiak, Rich. "Truman Capote: Addict and Genius." Rev. of Conversations With Capote by Lawrence Grobel. Bay Windows 25-30 May 1985: 23.

In his review, Grzesiak writes that "if one fantasizes that addiction gives an artist extraordinary powers, Capote's painful life stands as a powerful counterargument" because alcoholism kills even geniuses like him.

256 Guinan, M.E., et al. "Heterosexual and Homosexual Patients with the Aquired Immunodeficiency Syndrome: A Comparison of Surveillance, Interview and Laboratory Data." Annal of Internal Medicine 100 (1984): 213-18.

In this study of 50 homosexual men with AIDS, 96% had used nitrites, 80% had used marijuana, 66% had used nasal cocaine, and 50% had used ethyl chloride. No questions were asked regarding alcohol use.

257 Guss, David A., Sven A. Norman, and Anthony S. Manoguerra. "Clinically Significant Methemoglobinemia

from Inhalation of Isobutyl Nitrite." American Journal of Emergency Medicine (January 1985): 46-7.

The authors report on a case of a 21 year old gay man who almost died from methemoglobinemia as a result of inhaling poppers.

258 H., Dick. "Alcoholism Took Him to Places Most of Us Will Never See...and He Recovered." RFD 28 (1981): 34-5.

Dick tells the story of his life which included an alcoholic mother, a murdered lover whom he was initially charged with killing, an unsuccessful suicide attempt which left him in the hospital for a year, the plans for a perfect suicide, and the alcoholic paralysis which forced him to "hit bottom." He concludes his story with the comment that: "I know for sure that there has been a power greater than myself that has lifted me, at the right time and the right place. It has worked through people."

259 H., Doug. "I Grew Up Alcoholic and Gay in a Small Southern Town..." RFD 28 (1981): 35.

The theme of Doug's brief account is that he "now know[s] that A.A. saved me from doing real harm to myself, maybe others too."

260 Hackney, Edwin. "Gay/Lesbian Co-Dependency and Self-Oppression." Seventh National Lesbian/Gay Health Conference and Fourth National AIDS Forum, Washington, DC, March 1986.

Hackney's thesis is that "Careful attention needs to be given to the identification of co-dependence as a serious mental health disorder associated with the illness of chemical dependence among gay men and lesbians."

261 Hadden, Samuel B. "Group Psychotherapy." Gay

American History. Ed. Jonathan Katz. New York: Harper and Row, 1976. 186-87.

Hadden writed that "The alcoholic, through the psychiatrically sound program of Alcoholics Anonymous, has contributed much to the solution and understanding of alcoholism at little cost to the public. I am sure that the homosexual who consciously seeks help will not plead for special legislation to make it easier for him to continue his maladjusted pattern of sexual behavior when once it is demonstrated to him that he can regain a position in society through effective psychotherapy." The article was originally published in 1957.

262 Hagerty, Richard J. "Perception of the Gay Male Towards the Responsiveness of Alcoholic Treatment Centers to the Gay Person." Saddleback College. Unpublished paper, 2 April 1983.

"The purpose of this study will be to recognize and explore the problems that are particular to the Gay Community in treating and helping in the recovery of the Gay Alcoholics. It is further hoped to create an awareness that there is a need for changes in attitudes within the treatment centers, agencies and the Gay Community, so that help can be made available."

263 ---. "Recovery of Gay Alcoholics within a Treatment Modality." Saddleback College, unpublished paper, 1983.

The emphasis in this paper is on homophobia both within society and within the treatment community.

264 Haight-Ashbury Free Medical Clinic. Shooting Up and Your Health. San Francisco: Haight-Ashbury Free Medical Clinic, nd.

"Shooting up drugs can be hazardous to your health. This leaflet gives basic information about these health hazards, what you can do to reduce your risk, and where you can go for medical help [in the San Francisco area]." Although the pamphlet does not address homosexuality specifically, a section on AIDS is included.

265 Hammond, D.C., G.Q. Jorgensen, and D.M. Ridgeway. "Sexual Adjustments of Female Alcoholics." unpublished manuscript, 1979.

This manuscript is cited in Sharon Wilsnack's "Drinking, Sexuality, and Sexual Dysfunction."

266 Hanson, William and Wes Muchmore. _Coming Out Right: A Guide for the Gay Male_. Boston: Alyson Publications, 1982.

The book includes a chapter on "Recreational Drug Use" in which the authors discuss the affects of various non-alcoholic drugs. Recreational use is stressed and abuse is repeatedly warned against. The authors conclude that "If dope is to be part of your life, you must remain strong and keep its influence weak, no more than a pleasant diversion. Drugs will not solve life's problems."

267 Harms, Ernest. "Group Psychotherapy and Abstinence." _Gay American History_. Ed. Jonathan Katz. New York: Harper and Row, 1976. 183-84.

Originally published as "Homo-Anonymous" in a 1953 issue of _Diseases of the Nervous System_, Harms suggests using a theraputic principle based on Alcoholics Anonymous to cure homosexual activity.

268 Hart, H.H. "Personality Factors in Alcoholism." _Archives Neurological Psychiatry_ 24 (1930): 116-34.

In his study of 30 alcoholic patients, five of whom were women, Hart concluded that "on considering the group as a whole, there seemed little evidence of any important or overt homosexual tendency."

269 Harte, K. Lorrain. [pseud]. Rev. of A Woman Like You. By Rachel V. NALGAP News 7.4 (1986): 7.

Harte is favorably impressed with Rachel V's book.

270 Hastings, P. "Alcohol and the Lesbian Community: Changing Patterns of Awareness." The Drinking and Drug Practices Surveyor 18 (1982): 3-7.

Hastings explains that the lesbian community has increased its awareness of alcoholism in recent years.

271 "HATS Alcoholism Program Funded." Gay Community News 10 December 1979: 10.

The article is cited in The Alternative Press Index 11.4 (1979): 2.

272 Hauer, Laurie and Tom Smith. "AIDS and Substance Abuse: A Plan for Prevention, Education, Evaluation, Treatment, and Funding." San Francisco: San Francisco General Hospital Department of Public Health, 1983.

In their statement of the problem, the authors make note of the high incidence of alcoholism in gay men.

273 Haven, Martha Jane. "Alcoholism and Self Esteem Among Women With a Female Sex Object Preference." Dissertation. California School of Professional Psychology, Los Angeles, CA, 1981.

The research investigated the self-esteem levels of non-alcoholic lesbians, presently alcoholic lesbians receiving in-patient treatment for alcoholism, presently alcoholic lesbians receiving out-patient treatment for alcoholism, and recovering lesbians.

274 Haverkos, Harry W., et al. "Disease Manifestation Among Homosexual Men with Acquired Immunodeficiency Syndrome (AIDS): A Possible Role of Nitrites in Kaposi's Sarcoma." Sexually Transmitted Diseases October-December 1985: 103-8.

The authors found a high incidence of drug abuse in the 87 homosexual men whom they studied. Statistics documenting the drugs taken are given. Fifty-eight percent of the men used five or more different street drugs.

275 Hawkins, James L. "Lesbianism and Alcoholism." Alcohol Problems in Women and Children. Ed. Milton Greenblatt and Mark Schuckit. New York: Grune and Stratton, 1976: 137-54.

Hawkins begins his article by reviewing the literature on lesbianism, society's attitudes toward homosexuals, and myths about homosexuality. His discussion of the lesbian alcoholic makes much use of Lilene Fifield's "On My Way Nowhere".

276 Hay, Henry. "Founding the Mattachine Society." Gay American History. Ed. Jonathan Katz. New York: Harper and Row, 1976: 406-20.

The Mattachine Society's service function was compared to Alcoholics Anonymous.

277 "He Sets His Own Stage." The Way Back. 1981. Whitman-Walker Clinic: Washington, DC, 1982. 57-64.

A gay man tells how AA helped him "pick up the pieces and move on."

278 Hedges, Carole. "Aspects of Grief in Alcoholism and Sexual Awareness and the Role of the Therapist." National Gay/Lesbian Health Education Foundation Conference, New York, NY, 16-19 June 1984.

Hedges applies the grieving process to the alcoholic who stops drinking. The implications of this process for homosexuals is emphasized.

279 Heller, Marge. "Lesbian Alcoholism: Effects of Societal Pressure and the Road to Recovery." Paper in

Partial Completion of the Training Program for Alcoholism Counseling, The Institute for Alcohol Studies at South Oaks, 26 April 1983.

The paper explains the "pressures created by society such as ostracism, rejection of one's family, and general lack of acceptance" which lesbians face and how these problems affect their treatment by alcoholism professionals.

280 Helquist, Michael. Poppers, Your Health, and AIDS: Can You Afford the Risk? San Francisco: Substance Abuse and AIDS Task Force, 1985.

This brochure gives the scientific picture of the poppers/AIDS connection. Questions concerning popper use/abuse are answered and information is given on how one can cut back on or refuse poppers.

281 Hendrich, Suzanne. "On My Two Year Birthday." Out From Under. Ed. Jean Swallow. San Francisco: Spinsters, Ink, 1983. 8-10.

A poem that expresses the changes after two years of sobriety.

282 Hendrix, Kathleen. "Lesbian Alcoholics: Climbing Up From Nowhere." Los Angeles Times 16 July 1975. sec. 4. 1+.

This article revolves around the case histories of lesbian alcoholics.

283 ---. "Lesbian Alcoholics: Therapy Centers Point the Way Back." Los Angeles Times 17 July 1975. sec 4: 1+.

The article focuses on the Los Angeles Women's Alcoholism Center.

284 Heymont, George. "Fame, Monumental Talent, Alcoholism, and Homosexuality." Alcoholism Magazine (November-December 1983): 54-5.

A brief article about a gay alcoholic in a successful position.

285 Hilalgo, H., T.L. Peterson, and N.J. Woodman, eds. Lesbian and Gay Issues: A Resource for Social Workers. Silver Springs, MD: National Association of Social Workers, 1985.

Information is included concerning alcoholism.

286 Hoffman, Martin. The Gay World: Male Homosexuality and the Social Creation of Evil. New York: Basic, 1968.

Hoffman makes reference to alcohol use in gay bars.

287 Hoffman, W.M., ed. Gay Plays. New York: Avon, 1979.

This anthology includes Robert Patrick's "T-Shirts."

288 Holland, Flint. [pseud] Secret in a Bottle: The Cause and Cure of Alcoholism. New York: Pageant, 1952.

In novelized form, the author attempts "to expose bluntly the ghost behind the alcoholic." The "ghost" Holland identifies is latent homosexuality.

289 Holleran, Andrew. "The Lady With the Dog: What am I Doing in Pittsburgh, Waiting for Someone to Come Into the Baths?" Christopher Street 8.9 (1985): 17-20.

In writing about his visit to Pittsburgh, Holleran mentions that "gay AA groups" are listed on the Gay Switchboard hotline.

290 Homiller, Jonica D. Women and Alcohol: A Guide for State and Local Decision Makers. Washington, D.C.: Council of State Authorities, Alcohol and Drug Problems Association of North America, 1972.

Studies relating to alcoholism in the lesbian community are described.

291 *Homosexual Alcoholic: AA's Message of Hope to Gay Men and Women*. Center City, MN: Hazelden, 1980.

This pamphlet addresses the issue of honesty as it relates to homosexuals in AA as well as answers questions about homosexual groups within AA.

292 Hooker, Evelyn. "The Case of El: A Biography." *Journal of Projective Techniques and Personality Assessment* 25 (1961): 252-67.

Hooker presents a case study of El, a gay alcoholic.

293 Hoover, James. "Pride Institute: Breaking New Ground for Recovery." *Bay Windows* 4.21 (1986): 1+.

A discussion of Pride Institute, "the first in-patient chemical treatment facility for gays and lesbians."

294 ---. "Recovery: The Other Side of Addiction." *Bay Windows* 4.21 (1986): 1+.

A discussion of recovery based on interviews with three gay men and three lesbians.

295 "'Inclusive, Never Exclusive?'" *Box 1980* ["The Grapevine"] 38.12 (1980): 41.

This letter mentions that "a woman was voted out [of an AA meeting] because she was a lesbian.

296 "In Sobriety, You Get Life: An Interview with Celinda Cantu." *Out from Under*. Ed. Jean Swallow. San Francisco: Spinsters, Ink, 1983. 84-92.

"Celina Cantu, 31, works for Alameda County (CA) as a drug program consultant, helping set funding priorities to ensure that treatment in the county is accessible." Her comments focus on recovery as a community process and on recovery for non-white women.

297 Introduction to the Newtown Alano Club. Chicago: New Town Alano Club, 1985.

A description of services at the New Town Alano Club, which caters to the needs of lesbian/gay alcoholics.

298 Irvine, Janice. "Secrets of Fear, Shame and Love: Children of Alcoholic Parents." Gay Community News 11 August 1984: 8-9.

Irvine begins with a strong description of adult children of alcoholics. But, the last half of the article is devoted to a discussion of why she is philosophically opposed to AA and Al-Anon as well as the disease concept of alcoholism.

299 Israelstam, Stephen and Sylvia Lambert. "Homosexuality as a Cause of Alcoholism: A Historical Review." The International Journal of the Addictions 18.8 (1983): 1085-107.

The authors write that "In this paper we attempt to delineate the various aspects of the theory [that homosexuality causes alcoholism] and review work of psychiatrists and social scientists whose work supported or refuted the idea of a causal relationship."

300 Israelstam, Stephen, Sylvia Lambert, and Gustave Oki. "Poppers, A New Recreational Drug Craze." Canadian Psychiatric Association Journal 23.7 (1978): 493-95.

A brief description of the role poppers play in the gay community. Special emphasis is placed on how poppers are used during sexual activity.

301 ---. "Use of Isobutyl Nitrite as a Recreational Drug." British Journal of Addiction 73.3 (1978): 319-20.

Summary of findings from interviews of 150 isobutyl nitrite users.

302 "Issues of Sexuality and Alcoholism." Observer: News from the Johnson Institute 8.3 (1986): 5-6.

A summary of a talk Dana G. Finnegan gave at the Johnson Institute in which she openly discussed her lesbianism, alcohol addiction, and recovery from alcoholism.

303 "It's a Wonder We Have Sex At All: An Interview with JoAnn Gardner-Loulan." Out From Under. Ed. Jean Swallow. San Francisco: Spinsters, Ink, 1983. 93-101.

"JoAnn Gardner-Loulan, [a] 34 [year old co-alcoholic], is a therapist in private practice. The interview focuses on co-alcoholism.

304 J., P. "Acceptance is a Two-Way Street." Box 1980 ["The Grapevine"] April 1985: 29-31.

J.P. discusses the lack of understanding that sometimes exists between homosexual members of AA and non-homosexual members. The thesis of the article is that homosexuals need to practice acceptance, too.

305 Jaffe, H.W., et al. "National Case-Control Study of Kaposi's Sarcoma and Pneumocystis Carnii Pneumonia in Homosexual Men: Part 1. Epidemiologic Results." Annals of Internal Medicine 99.2 (1983): 145-51.

"Certain aspects of a lifestyle shared by a sub-group of the male homosexual population [including a high number of sex partners and use of illicit substances] are associated with an increased risk of Kaposi's Sarcoma and pneumocystis pneumonia."

306 James, W. "Maudlin Melodrama." Gay Community News 19 February 1983: 25.

The article is listed under the "Alcoholism" category in The Alternative Press Index 15.1 (1983): 2.

307 Jay, Karla and Allen Young. After You're Out: Personal Experiences of Gay Men and Lesbian Women. 1975. New York: Pyramid Books, 1977.

The book includes a chapter on alcohol use and abuse in the homosexual community.

308 John. "I Had Become a Co-Alcoholic..." RFD 28 (1981): 32-3.

A brief discussion of how his lover's sobriety affected their relationship. In part, John writes: "My lover and I were affected by each other. I, by his disease; and he by my attitudes and behaviors toward his drinking and from dealing with an alcoholic since childhood."

309 Johnson, Sandra. "Helping Lesbian Alcoholics." Off Our Backs 10.6 (1980): 7.

Johnson gives an overview of a talk given by Thomas Ziebold. She lists the Washington Gay Council on Drinking Behavior as a resource.

310 ---. Rev. of The Invisible Alcoholics. By Mariam Sandmaier. Off Our Backs 10.3 (1980): 24.

"One major fact that emerges from her work is the great diversity among women who abuse alcohol." The only two faults are that Sandmaier does not give a plan of action for confronting the problem of alcoholism nor does she present any information on fetal alcohol syndrome. "Nevertheless, the range of topics covered in this clearly written book is extensive, and even a lengthy review cannot do the book justice."

311 ---. Rev. of The Way Back. By the Gay Council on Drinking Behavior. Off Our Backs 12.8 (1982): 27.

Although Johnson is pleased with the book, she is disappointed that the book doesn't say how AA changed the peoples' lives. "There is more struggle in obtaining and maintaining a drug-free life than is recorded in these pages." She says that a description of the community support needed to maintain sobriety among lesbians is also missing. "Hopefully, the stories will be a turning point for someone who needs to hear a lesbian talk about her alcohol problem." The review includes addresses and phone numbers for the Gay Council on Drinking Behavior, AA, and Women for Sobriety.

312 Jones, Ernest. "Recent Advances in Psycho-Analysis." *International Journal of Psychoanalysis* 1 (1920): 161-85.

Jones writes: "I may remind you of the essential part that repressed homosexuality has been found to play in the causation of chronic alcoholism, of drug habits, and of paranoia..."

313 Jones, Karen A., J. David Latham, and Marcie D. Jenner. "Social Environment Within Conventional Alcoholism Treatment Agencies as Perceived by Gay and Non-Gay Recovering Alcoholics: A Preliminary Report." National Alcoholism Forum, Seattle, WA, 3 May 1980.

A preliminary report of the Orange County California Gay Alcoholic Needs Assessment Project.

314 Jørgensen, Karl A. and Sven-Olov Lawesson. Letter. "Amyl Nitrite and Kaposi's Sarcoma in Homosexual Men." *New England Journal of Medicine* 30 September 1982: 1893-94.

The authors conclude that they "find it appropriate to suggest that amyl nitrite may cause Kaposi's Sarcoma in homosexual men."

315 Judd, J.D. "Alcoholism and the Gay Community." Thesis. California State University, Hayward, 1977.

The thesis is cited in C. Vourakis' "Homosexuals in Treatment."

316 Judd, Tama Dawn. "A Survey of Non-Gay Alcoholism Treatment Agencies and Services Offered for Gay Women and Men." A Multicultural View of Drug Abuse. Ed. David E. Smith et al. Cambridge: Schenkman, 1978. 539-47.

Judd surveys staff attitudes in treatment centers located in the San Francisco Bay area.

317 Kalishman, et al. "Sisters and the Plague." Off Our Backs 3.3 (1972): 28.

The article is cited under the alcoholism category in The Alternative Press Index 4.4 (1972): 2.

318 Kallan, Sim. "1973 I Decided to Give Up Shooting Dope." Out From Under. Ed. Jean Swallow. San Francisco: Spinsters, Ink, 1983. 44-5.

A poem about the risks of heroin and benefits of not shooting dope.

319 Katz, Jonathan, ed. Gay American History: Lesbians and Gay Men in the USA. New York: Harper and Row, 1976.

The book includes Samuel B. Hadden's "Group Psychotherapy," Ernest Harms' "Group Psychotherapy and Abstinence," and Henry Hay's "Founding the Mattachine Society."

320 Kelleher, Jim. "Alcoholism and Sexuality." National Clergy Council on Alcoholism, Chicago, 16-20 June 1986.

Kelleher uses his own alcoholism and homosexuality for examples as to how clergy can address the needs of homosexuals, alcoholics, and homosexual alcoholics. The printed version of the talk includes 11 pages of questions and answers. A tape is also available.

321 Kikel, Rudy. "Alcoholism in the Gay and Lesbian Community: A Look at Three Men Who Are Young, Gay, and Sober Today." Bay Windows 25-30 May 1985: 1+.

The three biographies are intended to be "three colorations, three lenses, if you will, by means of which we may look unassisted in envisioning a phenomenon the nature of which is always to camouflage itself, to conceal its shape and texture." In spite of the title, lesbian alcoholics are not mentioned.

322 Kinsey, Barry A. The Female Alcoholic: A Social Psychological Study. Springfield, IL: Charles C. Thomas, 1966.

Seven percent of Kinsey's sample named homosexuality as a cause of their drinking.

323 ---. "Psychological Factors in Alcoholic Women from a State Hospital Sample." American Journal of Psychiatry 124.10 (1968): 1463-66.

The abstract included with the article reads: "The author compares the findings of a state hospital study of 46 alcoholic women of low socio-economic status with results of several other studies of alcoholic women from different socio-economic and cultural backgrounds." Homosexuality was listed as one of the physiological factors related to the onset of alcoholism.

324 Knight, Robert. "The Dynamics of Treatment of Chronic Alcohol Addiction." The Bulletin of the Menninger Clinic 1 (1937): 234.

The pathology of alcoholism was thought to be repressed homosexuality, however, Knight found that women were less likely than men to turn to alcohol when confronting their homosexuality.

325 Knowles, Janice. "The Pride Behind Pride Institute." ARC Circular 3.1 (March 1986): 1+.

A description of Pride Institute, the first treatment facility for lesbians and gay men.

326 Komaridis, Kathleen Gates. "Lesbians Do Exist: The Myths and Realities of Working with Alcoholic Lesbians--A Presentation for the Non-Gay Professional." National Alcoholism Forum, Seattle, 3 May 1980.

Komaridis presents 10 myths that therapists should be aware of when working with lesbian clients.

327 Koplin, Jim. "Healthy Perspectives: Alcohol and Gay People." Comma-dot 1.1 (1985): 16+.

Koplin provides a statistical overview of the problem of alcoholism in the homosexual community.

328 Korcok, Milan. AIDS and Chemical Dependency: What the Treatment Community Needs to Know. Pompano Beach, FL: Health Communications, Inc., 1985.

A good pamphlet which presents the link between AIDS and chemical dependency. An explanation of AIDS and the lack of any threat which it presents to health workers is also discussed.

329 Kraehe, Claudia. "Breath of a Gorilla Girl (A Fairy Tale)." Out From Under. Ed. Jean Swallow. San Francisco: Spinsters, Ink, 1983. 3-7.

A "fairy tale" about a gorilla girl who grew up to be an alcoholic but is able to get sober with the help of other gorillas.

330 Kramer, Norman D. "The Gay Man's Drug: Poppers." Advocate 30 June 1976: 22-3.

Kramer writes that his intent is to "Provide impartial and factual information which will better equip readers to make informed decisions about the use of this readily available substance [amyl nitrite]."

331 Kreideler, Bill. "Help is Available for Gay Alcoholcs: GLCS Lends a Supportive Ear." Bay Windows 25-30 May 1985: 13-14.

In discussing the work of Gay Lesbian Counseling Services in Boston, focus is on helping lesbian alcoholics.

332 Krinsky, C.M. and J.J. Michaels. "A Survey of 100 Sex Offenders Admitted to the Boston Psychiatric Hospital." Journal of Criminal Psychopathology 2.2 (1940): 199-201.

The article makes connections between homosexuality and alcohol abuse.

333 Kristi. "Lesbians and Alcoholism." Lesbian Connection 1.3 (1975). 4-6.

Kristi makes general comments on alcoholism before explaining the stages of alcoholism as they relate to lesbians. See Catherine's "Letter" for response.

334 Kus, Robert J. "Alcoholics Anonymous and Gay American Men." unpublished.

"The article explores the gay alcoholic man in relation to AA as well as how professionals may be supportive of the gay AA member. Finally, some suggestions about how rural gay alcoholic men might be better served are provided." Currently under review for publication.

335 ---. "The Alcoholics Anonymous Sponsor and Gay American Men." 32nd International Institute on the Prevention and Treatment of Alcoholism, Budapest, June, 1986.

The paper explores the necessity of sponsors, how sponsors are chosen, the perceived qualities and duties of the sponsor, and strategies for letting go of one's sponsor.

336 ---. "From Grounded Theory to Clinical Practice: Cases from Gay Studies Research." From Grounded Theory to Clinical Practice: Qualitative Research in Nursing. Ed. W.C. Scenitz and J.M. Swanson. Menlo Park, CA: Addison-Wesley, 1986. 227-40.

Kus explains the stages in the coming out process and how knowledge of those stages can be applied to work with gay clients. In the case studies, alcoholism is discussed.

337 ---. "Gay Alcoholism and Non-Acceptance: The Critical Link." Edu-Center for Nurses for "Nursing Research--Hawaii '85" Honolulu, HA, 1985.

This paper advances the argument that the entiology of alcoholism in the gay community is not related to gay bars.

338 ---. "The Higher Power and Gay American Men: A Study in Sobriety." Special Program in Honor of Dr. Gordon Browder, Missoula, MT 25-26 April 1986.

Similar to Kus' "Gay Alcoholism and Non-Acceptance."

339 ---. "Sex and Sobriety: The Gay Experience." National Symposium of Nursing Research, San Francisco, November 14-16, 1985.

Kus concludes: "With knowledge of how sobriety positively affects sexual enjoyment and performance in gay American men, nurses can help dispel possible fears held by gay alcoholic men who haven't yet chosen and lived soberly, fears and myths that sex sober will be boring, that they won't enjoy it as much, and the like."

340 ---. "Stages of Coming Out: An Ethnographic Approach." Western Journal of Nursing Research 7.2 (1985): 177-98.

AA is mentioned.

341 L., B. ''You Mean, Just Let Anybody In?'" Box 1980 ["The Grapevine"] September 1976: 26-9.

B.L. describes a 1945 incident of a man who showed up at AA in order to discuss the AA's Third Tradition: "The only requirement for AA membership is a desire to stop drinking." The man had described himself as "a jailbird, mental case, narcotics addict, homosexual, and alcoholic."

342 L., Barry. "Historical Perpective: Homosexual Men and Women in AA." International AA Conference, Montreal, June 1985.

Although no formal paper is available, a tape of this lecture exists.

343 L., K[el]. "Here I Am." Box 1980 ["The Grapevine"] January 1980: 13-4.

Kel, a lesbian, discusses her higher power whom she calls Herhim. But her thesis is that straights in AA can help homosexual alcoholics.

344 Labataille, L. "Amyl Nitrite Employed in Homosexual Relations." Medical Aspects of Human Sexuality 9:122 (1975).

This article is cited in Larry Siegell's "Popping and Snorting Volatile Nitrites."

345 [Lampman, Cindy] "'Ramblings' With the Editor: A Commentary of Sorts." Unitarian Universalist Lesbian/Gay Word April/May 1983.

Lampman writes that as she worked to prepare the special issue on alcoholism, she learned "that the majority of gay alcoholics...considered themselves to be alcoholics--period--and that their sexuality had little or no bearing on that fact; that they didn't start drinking because of it."

346 Lane, Linda. "Lesbian Alcoholism Group Forms." Big Mama Rag 6.8 (1978): 1.

After giving some of her own drinking history and telling of the problems lesbian alcoholics suffer in traditional treatment programs, Lane describes LUNA (Lesbians United to "Nip" Alcoholism), "a newly formed support group for lesbian alcoholics, drinking or recovering, and for their friends, lovers or significant others."

347 Lange, Gary. "Treating the Significant Other of the Chemically Dependent Gay/Lesbian." First International Lesbian/Gay Health Conference, New York, June 1984.

This paper is cited in Edwin Hackney's "Gay/Lesbian Co-Dependency and Self-Oppression."

348 Langone, John and Delores de Nobrega Langone. Women Who Drink. Reading, MA: Addison-Wesley, 1980.

The authors make three points: (1) Alcoholism professionals frequently want to treat a woman's lesbianism rather than her alcoholism. (2) A lesbian alcoholic has a quadruple alienation from society. She is an alcoholic, a woman, a homosexual, and a female homosexual in a gay culture dominated by men. (3) AA generally does not meet the needs of the lesbian alcoholic because homosexuality is often difficult to face for most AA members.

349 Lanzaratta, Philip. "Surviving AIDS." Christopher Street 8.9 (1985): 30-35.

In this follow-up article to his "Why Me?," drugs are listed as part of the past and Lanzaratta describes his wholistic approach to health.

350 ---. "Why Me?" Christopher Street 6.3 (1982): 15-6.

In telling about his AIDS diagnosis, the author answers the rhetorical question, "Is there life after drugs?"

Although his answer is yes, he explains that he still uses some drugs recreationally, but to a much lesser extent than he previously did.

351 Larkin, Trisha. "The Meaning of Rapture." Out From Under. Ed. Jean Swallow. San Francisco: Spinsters, Ink, 1983. 148-50.

A personal story of recovery.

352 "Laurel's Story." The Sentinel 6 March 1981: 4.

An interview with a 30 year old lesbian alcoholic.

353 Lauritsen, John and Hank Wilson. Death Rush: Poppers and AIDS. New York: Pagan Press, 1986.

This book includes an annotated bibliography on nitrite inhalants as well as chapters on "Poppers and AIDS," and "The Poppers Industry and Its Influence" as well as three appendixes which focus on drugs as a co-factor in AIDS.

354 Leavenworth, Roger and Tom McGraw. "Report of the Substance Abuse Task Force." Developing a Positive Lesbian/Gay Identity Conference, Detroit, MI 4 May 1986.

The report examines the way in which to deal with the growing problem of chemical addiction within Detroit's lesbian and gay community.

355 "Lesbian and Gay Alcoholics." Community Dialogue 7 (1980): 2-4.

The article includes excerpts from "Gay? Drinking Problem?" and Don Michael's "Sober, Clean, and Gay." A resource list is also included.

356 Lesbian or Gay and Alcoholic. New York: International Advisory Council for Homosexual Men and Women in Alcoholics Anonymous, nd.

The book poses questions about homosexuality and alcoholism, the twenty question test that is often used to "determine" alcoholism, and the twelve steps of AA. Different titles are listed on each side of the pamphlet. The other title is Gay or Lesbian and Alcoholic?

357 Lesbians United to "Nip" Alcoholism. "What? Another Closet?" np: LUNA, nd.

A two page fact sheet which explains the politics of addiction.

358 Levine, Jacob. "The Sexual Adjustment of Alcoholics--A Clinical Study of a Selected Sample." Quarterly Journal of Studies on Alcohol 16 (1955): 675-80.

Levine claims that his findings "are consistent with the psychoanalytic hypothesis that the alcoholic has a basic homosexual problem. Addiction to alcohol is presumed to be one way of dealing with the conflict which is largely unconscious."

359 Lewis, Collins, Marcel Saghir, and Eli Robins. "Drinking Patterns in Homosexual and Heterosexual Women." Journal of Clinical Psychiatry 43.7 (1982): 277-79.

The abstract which is included with the article reads: "The lifetime prevalance of heavy and problem drinking was found to be significantly higher in a sample of homosexual women (N=57) compared to a demographically matched sample of heterosexual women (N=43). This prevalence of excessive drinking is not explained by personality traits, psychiatric diagnosis, gender identity, history of frequenting gay bars, or family history of alcoholism."

360 Lewis, N.D.C. "Psychiatric Resultants of Alcoholism and Mental Disease." Quarterly Journal of Studies on Alcohol 2 (1941): 293-311.

During acute alcoholic hallucinosis, male patients were apt to hear voices that accused them of homosexual practices. Females hear voices who accused them of loose conduct of a heterosexual nature.

361 Liberacki, Alex. [pseud] "Homemaking in an Unwelcoming Environment." <u>More Light Update</u> March 1985: 6-7.

The article is a response to Chris Glaser's "Making the World Safe for Diversity" (<u>More Light Update</u>, December 1984). Liberacki offers suggestions as to how homosexual Christian organizations have been welcoming the homosexual alcoholic.

362 ---. "Hope for the Community: Alcoholism is a Treatable Disease." Whitman-Brooks Developing a Positive Lesbian/Gay Identity Conference. Detroit, Michigan, 28 April 1985.

The paper focuses on what the lesbian/gay community can do to respond to alcoholism.

363 ---. "The Lives We Save May Be Our Own." East Lansing: Dignity/Region 5 Substance Abuse Task Force, 1985.

The paper is based on the remarks Liberacki made in his seminar, "Hope for the Community."

364 "Liberated Woman." <u>The Way Back</u>. 1981. Washington, D.C.: The Whitman-Walker Clinic, 1982. 65-74.

A Jewish woman tells about her period of liberation--as a lesbian and as a woman--after joining AA.

365 Lipman, Joanne. "Gay in the 80s" <u>Home News</u> 2-3 August 1981.

A series of articles on homosexuality that include Lipman's "Homosexual Teens Face Rough Path" and "Little Agreement on 'Cause' of Homosexuality."

366 ---. "Homosexual Teens Face Rough Path." The Home News 3 August 1981: A7.

Lipman writes that "In their desperate determination to hold back such a dominant part of their personalities, gay teens turn to drugs, alcohol, malicious 'fag-baiting'--and sometimes suicide."

367 ---. "Little Agreement on 'Cause' of Homosexuality." The Home News 2 August 1981: C1.

In a discussion of NAGAP, Lipman mentions the importance of helping homosexual alcoholics accept their sexuality.

368 Lohrenz, Leander J. et al. "Alcohol Problems in Several Midwestern Homosexual Communities." Journal of Studies on Alcohol 39 (1978): 159-63.

The summary provided with the article reads: "According to their scores on the Michigan Alcoholism Screening Test, close to one third of the homosexual men surveyed in four urban areas of Kansas were alcoholics."

369 Lolli, Giorgio. "Alcoholism and Homosexuality in Tennessee Williams' Cat On A Hot Tin Roof." Quarterly Journal of Studies on Alcohol 17 (1956): 543-53.

Lolli believes that: "Alcoholism and homosexuality represent a perverted and crippling solution to the fundamental problems of existence, expressed concretely and painfully felt in the dilemma of the body-mind relations." The review revolves around this thesis.

370 London, J. "Alcoholism and Homosexuality." University of Washington School of Social Work. May 1975.

This paper is an overview of psychological literature and personal observations. Citations are poorly documented.

371 Loucks, Charles C. and Gerald J. Higgins. "The Gay Alcoholic: A Problem of Parallel Stigmas." National Council on Alcoholism Forum, Seattle, May 1980.

The authors identify how the stigmas of being homosexual, alcoholic (and, for women, lesbians) affect treatment. Solutions for the internalized homophobia of the individual gay/lesbian alcoholic are proposed.

372 Loulan, JoAnn. Lesbian Sex. San Francisco: Spinsters, Ink, 1984.

Loulan includes a chapter on "Sex and Sobriety" in which she covers such issues as the body and emotions during sex and recovery. The co-addict and sexual issues with the addict and co-addict are mentioned. Exercises are suggested to help the lesbian couple deal with recovery.

373 "Lovers and Other Co-Alcoholics." RFD 28 (1981): 31.

The theme of this article is that "Denial eventually traps the alcoholic's lover, or others who may be emotionally involved, into playing the same game....Under the constant onslaught of blame, the lover eventually reacts as the alcoholic against the projected guilt and anxiety and the lover's own fears of social rejection." Denial, and how to deal with it, are discussed.

374 "L.U.N.A." Big Mama Rag 6.8 (1978): 1.

A description of LUNA (Lesbians United to "Nip" Alcoholism), a support group for lesbian alcoholics, their lovers, and friends.

375 "LUNA: The Politics of Sobriety." Big Mama Rag 7.11 (1979): 10+.

The article explains that LUNA (Lesbians United to "Nip" Alcoholism) believes that alcoholism is a feminist issue.

376 Lundgren, William S. and Carol S. Flood. "A Comparative Look at Gay, Mixed, and Straight Therapy Groups for Substance Abusers." Pennsylvania Department of Health, Drug and Alcohol Abuse Conference, Lancaster, PA 13 October 1982.

The authors conclude "that the ideal situation for gay clients would be a segregated [homosexual only] group." Heterosexual and gay therapists should be included in such a group.

377 Lurie, Louis A. and Carl H. Jonas. "Causes of Homosexuality." Sexology 11.12 (1945): 743-46.

Alcoholism is mentioned in the article.

378 Lynch, Beverly. "Felicita G." The Lavender Herring (nd): 61-69.

A social worker records the problems facing a Spanish Lesbian drug abuser.

379 M., Andy. "The Joy of Living..." RFD 28 (1981): 32.

Andy reflects on his "bottom" and the life he has today.

380 M., F. "A Dykes Drunkalogue." Bay Windows 25-30 May 1985: 12.

F.M. an alcoholic lesbian tells the story of her addiction and recovery.

381 M., Susan. "Living With an Alcoholic." RFD 28 (1981): 33-4.

Susan, the only child in an alcoholic home, tells of the fears and insecurity when she fell in love with a recovering alcoholic. She writes that "I decided to go to Al-Anon as a last resort. After 8 months of living with an alcoholic, a sober alcoholic, my life had become unmanageable. The program is slowly and surely putting things into a workable perspective."

382 MacLean, J. Rev. of Out From Under. By Jean Swallow. Advocate 20 March 1984: 48.

Although she does have some reservations about the validity of Swallow's statistics, MacLean is impressed with the book. She comments: "I've done my share of complaining about the moralism of those who make a big deal about 'clean and sober' space at women's events. After reading these brave stories, no more. The way the mainstream and lesbian cultures both assume that things go better with alcohol is, for some women, literally a matter of life and death."

383 Machover, S., F.S. Puzzo, K. Machover, and F. Plumeau. "Clinical and Objective Studies of Personality Variables in Alcoholism: An Object Study of Homosexuality in Alcoholism." Quarterly Journal of Studies on Alcohol 20 (1959): 528-42.

"Two hypotheses generated in the course of clinical studies were tested: (1) that homosexual trends are more prevalent among male alcoholics than non-alcoholics, and (2) that homosexual trends are more in evidence among remitted than unremitted alcoholics." The first hypothesis was not confirmed. The second was.

384 MacPherson, Gary A. "The Homosexual Homophobia of the Gay Alcoholic as a Factor for Consideration in the Treatment of Alcoholism." Thesis. Hofstra University, Hempstead, New York, 1977.

MacPherson's thesis demonstrated in part that "being gay is in no way a deterrent to the maintenance of sobriety."

385 Madisen, C. "Mood Swings...Lesbian Theatre Group." Gay Community News 23 October 1982: 8.

The article is cited under the "Alcoholism" category in The Alternative Press Index 14.4 (1982): 2.

386 Mangual, Louis. "Management Issues With Homosexuality in an Adolescent Drug Treatment Program." A Multicultural View of Drug Abuse. Ed. David E. Smith, et al. Cambridge: Schenkman, 1978. 530-38.

Citing his own experiences as a gay, 16 year old, heroin addict as well as case studies from his patients, Mangual offers suggestions on how staff can deal with the adolescent homosexual who enters a recovery program. He believes that "the roles of drug abuse treatment and of the adolescent homosexual must be joined with the emphasis on the subject's ability to maintain a stable life free from drug abuse."

387 Marcelle, George. "Alcoholism and the Gay Community: The State of Knowledge Today." Third Annual National Lesbian and Gay Health Conference, San Francisco, June 1980.

A survey of papers and articles about alcoholism in the homosexual community. A summary of each citation is given. The focus is on those papers presented at the National Alcoholism Forum of the National Council on Alcoholism, Seattle, WA, May 1980.

388 Marden, Parker G. "Prevalence of Alcohol Abuse in the Gay Population of the United States." January 1980.

"The author's special interests center on social demography and the epidemiology of alcohol abuse." Marden concludes that: "The limited information on alcohol abuse in the gay population does not permit definitive conclusions, but it does suggest that the problem is a very serious one." Single copies of this unpublished paper are available from NCALI, Box 2345, Rockville, Maryland 20852. Order #: RPO 310.

389 Marie. "Je m'appelle Marie, et je suis un alcoolique (lesbienne)." Vous croyez-vous Différent? trans.

Service de la Littérature A.A. du Québec. Montreal: Service de la Littérature AA du Québec, 1979.

Translation of Mary's "My Name is Mary and I'm and Alcoholic (lesbian)."

390 Marklein, Carol and Gayle Ishlenfeld. "Alcoholism in the Lesbian Community." Nebraska Alcoholism Forum Newsletter 2 (May 1980): 1-2.

General overview of alcoholism in the lesbian community which concludes that alcohol use will not become abuse.

391 Marmor, Michael, et al. "Risk Factors for Kaposi's Sarcoma in Homosexual Men." The Lancet 15 May 1982: 1083-87.

In this study, multi-variate analysis indicated that use of amyl nitrite was an independent and statistically significant factor of Karposi's Sarcoma. The study was done on 20 gay Karposi's Sarcoma patients and 40 healthy controls.

392 Marschall, Rick. "Homosexual, Alcoholic Group Therapy: A Specialized Treatment." National Alcoholism Forum, Seattle, 4 May 1980.

After explaining how to set up a group for homosexual alcoholics, the author concludes that "The homosexual alcoholic group is an effective means for this population to adjust to the general stresses of integrating into society as a sober person, and at the same time beginning to face internalized homophobia which is a hidden and often unrecognized enemy and threat to the maintenance of sobriety.

393 Martin, Marcelina. "The Isolation of the Lesbian Alcoholic." Frontiers 4.2 (1979): 32-4.

Martin writes: A primary threat to psychological health, isolation is the cornerstone of alcoholism. For the lesbian, it is an unavoidable prelude to her lifestyle." The article focuses on how isolation can be overcome.

394 Martin, R.L., R. Cloninger, and S.B. Guze. "Female Criminality and the Prediction of Recidivism: A Prosective Six Year Follow-up." Archives of General Psychiatry 35.2 (1978): 207-14.

The authors found that "The most powerful predictors of recidivism were the diagnosis of drug dependence and antisocial personality, and a history of homosexuality."

395 Mary. "My Name is Mary and I'm an Alcoholic (lesbian)." Do You Think You're Different? New York: Alcoholics Anonymous, 1976. 17-8.

Mary stresses that the only requirement for AA membership is a desire to stop drinking.

396 Mathur-Wagh, Usha, et al. Letter. "Followup at 4 1/2 Years on Homosexual Men with Generalized Lymphadenopathy." New England Journal of Medicine 12 December 1985.

A history of moderate to heavy use of nitrite inhalants was an important co-factor for the patients who eventually developed AIDS.

397 ---. "Longitudinal Study of Persistent Generalized Lymphadenopathy in Homosexual Men: Relation to Acquired Immunodeficiency Syndrome." The Lancet 12 May 1984: 1033-38.

In this study of 42 homosexual or bisexual men, use of nitrite inhalants proved to be the most important factor distinguishing the eight patients who developed AIDS from those patients who did not develop it.

398 Mayer, Kenneth and James D'Eramo. "Poppers: A Storm Warning." Christopher Street 78 (1979): 46-9.

Mayer gives a summary of the medical knowledge about poppers and their possible role as a co-factor for contracting AIDS.

399 McDaniel, Judith. "First Tries Don't Always Work (Chapter Five)." Out From Under. Ed. Jean Swallow. San Francsico: Spinsters, Ink, 1983. 177-86.

The story of a policewoman's unsuccessful attempt to confront a fifteen year old girl about her problem with alcohol.

400 McGirr, Kevin J. "Alcohol Use and Abuse in the Gay Community: A View Toward Alternatives." After You're Out. By Karla Jay and Allen Young. 1975. New York: Pyramid Books, 1977. 277-88.

McGirr writes that: "Most discussion on the bars omits any discussion on the use and role of alcohol--this is what I would like to consider in this report." In the essay he considers alcoholism in the homosexual community including where lesbian and gay alcoholics can turn for assistance. A special section is titled "Alcoholism Amongst Gay Women." The text for the essay is based on a series of articles that appeared in Gay Community News, May 11, May 25, and June 8, 1974.

401 McKaen, Mauree. "Sexual Minority Human Service Agencies in the '80s: Where Do We Go From Here?" National Alcoholism Forum, Seattle, 4 May 1980.

Closing address of the Sexual Minorities Track.

402 McKirnan, David J. and Tina Johnson. "Life-Styles and Substance Abuse: Social Behavior, Attitudes and Alcohol--Drug Use in the Gay Community." unpublished.

The paper gives an overview of the methodology for a study "designed to measure alcohol and drug use/abuse within the gay community."

403 McNally, Emily B. and Dana G. Finnegan. "Jane Addams-Howard Brown Award Acceptance Speeches." The Official Newsletter of the National Coalition of Gay S[exually] T[ransmitted] D[isease] Services 5.1 (1983): 11-4.

In their speech accepting the Jane Addams-Howard Brown Award, McNally and Finnegan explain the problem of chemical addiction and the need for people to work together to address the issue.

404 ---. "Working Together: The National Association of Gay Alcoholism Professionals." Journal of Homosexuality 7.4 (1982): 101-4.

"The article briefly describes the formation of the National Association of Gay Alcoholism Professionals (NAGAP). It then discusses the need for education, information, and advocacy that prompted the development of NAGAP's goals."

405 McQueen, Robert I. Editorial. "An Insidious Disease: Alcoholism." Advocate 25 February 1974: 31.

McQueen argues that "the gay community must accept the responsibility of supporting these [gay recovery] programs and of making our community aware of their existence."

406 McPherson, Kay Marie. Letter. "New Group." Big Mama Rag 6.9 (1978).

McPherson tells how she is beginning to form a group of LUNA, Lesbians United to "Nip" Alcoholism.

407 McWhirter, David P. and Andrew M. Mattison. The Male Couple: How Relationships Develop. Englewood Cliffs: Prentice-Hall, 1984.

The authors comment that: "The widespread availability and use of drugs among gay men is usually socially accepted. As a consequence, a higher incidence of substance abuse and alcoholism has been recognized among gay men."

408 Mediplex. Gay and Lesbian Treatment at Mediplex. Newton, MA: Mediplex, [nd].

A description of the treatment philosophy at Mediplex Alcohol/Substance Abuse Treatment Facilities, 2101 Washington Street, Newton, MA 02162.

409 Meissner, Natasha and Herb Morton. Alcoholism in the Gay Community. Vancouver: Society for Education, Action, Research, and Counseling on Homosexuality, 1977.

This publication is cited in William Crawford's Homosexuality in Canada.

410 Member of Dignity/Region 5. Dignity and Recovery: A Gay Catholic's Story. East Lansing, MI: Dignity/Region 5 Substance Abuse Task Force, 1985.

The man tells the story of his life as an alcoholic and his recovery through AA. He also mentions how his involvement with Dignity helped his recovery and he offers suggestions on how Dignity and other organizations can address the needs of alcoholics.

411 Menninger, Karl A. Man Against Himself. New York: Harcourt-Brace and World, 1938.

Menninger found that: "Many alcoholics indulge in homosexual...relations only when they are drunk."

412 Mewington, N. Rev. Out From Under. Ed. Jean Swallow. Conditions 11 (1985): 190.

The review is cited in The Alternative Press Index 17.2 (1985): 3.

413 Michael, John. The Gay Drinking Problem...There is a Solution. Minneapolis: Compcare, 1976.

Michael tells his story of recovery from alcoholism and what organizations are available to help the homosexual alcoholic. The pamphlet would be primarily interesting to gay men.

414 ---. "The Gay Drinking Problem...There is a Solution." RFD 28 (1981): 29-30.

A reprint of the pamphlet of the same name.

415 ---. Sober, Clean, and Gay! Minneapolis: Compcare, 1977.

Michael discusses what recovering alcoholics mean by "program" as well as what such issues as attitude, acceptance, and spirituality have to do with recovery from alcoholism. A list of organizations which provide support for alcoholics and their family and friends is included.

416 Michaels, Don. "Reaching Out to Gay Alcoholics." 5th Freedom, May-June 1975: 17-8.

Summary of an interview with two gay men who attend (gay) AA meetings.

417 "Michael's Story." The Sentinel 6 March 1981: 4+.

An interview with Michael, a gay alcoholic with two years of sobriety.

418 Michener, Marian. "Three Glasses of Wine Have Been Removed from this Story: Excerpts from a Novel-in-Progress." Out From Under Ed. Jean Swallow. San Francisco: Spinsters, Ink, 1983. 204-20.

These pieces of fiction give an account of one woman's recovery from alcoholism.

419 Miller, Emanuel. "The Psycho-Pathological Aspects of Alcoholism." British Journal of Inebriation 28 (1931): 109-11.

Miller suggests that alcohol is used by an individual to seek escape from the struggle between homosexual sex and "normal" sex.

420 Miller, Merle. *On Being Different*. New York: Random House, 1971.

Miller discusses hiding his being alcoholic. He writes: "When I was a child...I loved Halloween. I never wanted to take off the mask; I wanted to wear it everywhere, night and day, always. And I suppose I still do. I have often used liquor, which is another kind of mask, and, more recently, pot."

421 Miller, Pam. "Recovery Services." *ACW Worth* 1.1 (1980): 2.

While explaining the work of the Alcoholism Center for Women, Miller writes that "we strive to provide services based on respect for the individual woman's dignity and self esteem, with particular concern for the needs of lesbians."

422 Moirai, Catherine Risingflame. "Four Poems in Search of a Sober Reader." *Sinister Wisdom* 19 (1982): 81-4.

The final stanza of poem four reads: "Watching a woman kill herself/by inches of a bottle/is not/a revolutionary act." Reprinted in Jean Swallow's *Out from Under*, pages 117-21.

423 Mongeon, John E. and Thomas O. Ziebold. "Preventing Alcohol Abuse in the Gay Community: Toward a Theory and Model." *Journal of Homosexuality* 7.4 (1982): 89-100.

"The model presented in this paper is based upon current research about successful prevention programs and uses accepted strategies tailored to the specific characteristics of the urban gay community. The basic premise of the model is that community self help is the most effective approach to alcohol and drug abuse prevention."

424 Moore, Jean, ed. *Roads to Recovery: A National Directory of Alcohol and Drug Addiction Treatment Centers.* New York: Macmillan, 1985.

The book includes an index of treatment centers for lesbian/gay clients.

425 Morales, Edward S. "Third World Gays and Lesbians: A Process of Multiple Identities." American Psychological Association, Anaheim, CA, 27 August 1983.

Morales points out that "Many gay research efforts have mostly focused on gay white males and white lesbians or lacked the report of data concerning the composition of Third World gays and lesbians in their sample." The conflicts between being a minority within a minority and how these conflicts can be resolved is emphasized. In chemcial addiction programs 80% of the counselors sampled for this project lacked the training to deal with ethnic clients.

426 Morales, Edward S. and Michael Graves. *Substance Abuse: Patterns and Barriers to Treatment for Gay Men and Lesbians in San Francisco.* San Francisco: Community Substance Abuse Services, San Francisco Department of Public Health, 1983.

A statistical analysis of the role of drugs in the lesbian/gay community. Very well documented.

427 Morris, Paul D. *Shadow of Sodom: Facing the Facts of Homosexuality.* Wheaton, IL: Tyndale House, 1978.

Morris observed the gay community while driving a taxi cab at night. Many of his comments involve activities associated with gay bars and alcoholic gays.

428 Moses, A. Elfin and Robert O. Hawkins, Jr. *Counseling*

Lesbian Women and Gay Men: A Life Issues Approach. St Louis: C.V. Mosby, 1982.

The authors claim that "the ready availabilty of alcohol in social situations combined with the pressures of a gay lifestyle may be sufficient to create a substance abuse problem in people who would not otherwise have one" and that to deal with alcoholism while trying to stay in the closet is almost impossible. The book also includes a lesbian alcoholic case study.

429 Moss, Andrew. "A Case-Control Study of Risk Factors for AIDS in San Francisco." Center for Disease Control AIDS Conference, Atlanta, 15 April 1985.

Moss found that of men who were antibody positive for HTLV-III, the heavier the use of poppers the more likely the patient was to acquire AIDS.

430 Moss, L. "Brenda Weathers: An Interview." Gaysweek 27 February 1978: 10.

The interview is cited in The Alternative Press Index 10.1 (1978): 2.

431 "Mother on the Run." The Way Back. 1981. Washington, DC: Whitman-Walker Clinic, 1982. 83-8.

As a diplomat's wife, the author says that she did not need to take a geographic cure for her alcoholism; it was done for her. Eventually, she joined AA and accepted both her alcoholism and her lesbianism.

432 Murry, Mary. "U[niversity] of I[owa] Professor Explains Homosexual Alcoholism." The Des Moines Register 14 February 1986. 3A

This newspaper article focuses on the work of Robert Kuss and his finding that gay bars cannot account for the incidence of alcoholism in gay men.

433 N., J. "'I Want to Belong.'" Box 1980 ["The Grapevine"] October 1977: 9-11.

J.N. discusses the harmful effects of anti-homosexual humor found in some AA meetings.

434 "NAGAP Begins." NAGAP Newsletter 1.1 (1979): 1.

A summary of the goals of the National Association of Gay Alcoholism Professionals.

435 "NAGAP Promotes Services to Gays." PLGTF Bulletin 3.9 (1981): 18.

A brief description of the National Association of Gay Alcoholism Professionals' goals.

436 Nancy. "Reaching the Lesbian Alcoholic." Summer School of Alcohol Studies and Alcohol and Sexuality Alumni Institute, Rutgers University, 1978.

Nancy explains that: "The lesbian alcoholic is a challenge to professionals in the treatment field. Generally alienated from straight society, she may be reluctant to approach a service agency for help. Once in an agency, she is hard to reach and extremely sensitive to negative attitudes." In her paper, Nancy presents suggestions as to how treatment facilities can meet the needs of lesbian clients.

437 Nardi, Peter M. "Alcohol Treatment and the Non-Traditional 'Family' Structures of Gays and Lesbians." Journal of Alcohol and Drug Education 27.2 (1982): 83-9.

Nardi discusses co-alcoholism in terms of the "significant other." Focus is placed on the unique dynamics of lesbian and gay "families."

438 ---. "Alcoholism and Homosexuality: A Theoretical Perspective." Journal of Homosexuality 7.4 (1982): 9-26.

"This paper analyzes the assumptions underlying the biological and genetic approaches, learning theory, psychoanalytic perspectives, and sociological models as they relate to alcoholism and homosexuality."

439 National Institute on Alcohol Abuse and Alcoholism and the National Clearinghouse for Alcohol Information. *Literature Search on Alcohol and the Immune System* The Effects of Alcohol on the Immune System Workshop, Bethesda, MD, 4-5 November 1985.

Includes abstracts of R.S. Ernst's "Characteristics of Gay Persons with Sexually Transmitted Diseases" and R.J. Frances' "Contracting AIDS as a means of Committing Suicide."

440 National Association of Gay Alcoholism Professionals. *Directory of Facilities and Services for Gay/Lesbian Alcoholics.* New York: National Association of Gay Alcoholism Professionas, 1981.

The directory was updated in 1986. For current biographical information, see Ron Vachon's "Directory of Facilities and Services."

441 "National Task Force to Study the Alcoholic Homosexual." *The Alcoholism Report* May 10, 1974: 5.

The article announced a task force formed by Brenda Weathers, Program Director at the Los Angeles Gay Community Services Center.

442 *New Beginnings: Chemical Dependency Program, Meeting the Special Needs of Gays and Lesbians.* Los Angeles: Century City Hospital, 2070 Century Park East, Los Angeles, CA 90067, [1986].

A description of the treatment services available for lesbian/gay clients at Century City Hospital.

443 Newell, Guy R., at al. "Risk Factor Analysis Among Men

Referred for Possible Acquired Immune Deficiency Syndrome." Preventive Medicine January 1985: 81-91.

The authors found that "the combination of cigarette smoking, marijuana use, and nitrite inhalation could predispose the lungs to opportunistic infections."

444 Newmeyer, John A. "The Sensuous Hippy: II. Gay/Straight Differences in Regard to Drugs and Sexuality." Drug Forum 6 (1977-78): 49-55.

The paper is based on a questionnaire study of the sexual practices and drug use of a sample of clients at the Haight-Ashbury Free Medical Clinic in San Francisco. Drug use and sexual practices were compared between homosexual and non-homosexual individuals.

445 "'The News' Editorializes Against Poppers." The Works 5.5 (1986): 13.

In mentioning an Indianapolis News editorial, the link between poppers and AIDS is mentioned.

446 "News Notes." Gay Community News 5 April 1980: 2.

The article is cited under the "Alcoholism" category in The Alternative Press Index 12.2 (1980): 2.

447 "News Notes." Gay Community News 12 April 1980: 2.

The article is cited under the "Alcoholism" category in The Alternative Press Index 12.2 (1980): 2.

448 "News Notes." Gay Community News 26 April 1980: 2.

The article is cited under the "Alcoholism" category in The Alternative Press Index 12.2 (1980): 2.

449 Nicholson, Stella. "Chemically Dependent Families: Roles, Rules, and Relationships." NALGAP First National Conference, Chicago, September 1985.

The paper is cited in Edwin Hackney's "Gay/Lesbian Co-Dependency."

450 "No Place to Hide." The Way Back. 1981. Washington, D.C.: Whitman-Walker Clinic, 1982. 7f.

Story of a gay man who found that geographic cures don't cure alcoholism, but AA does.

451 Noble, Elaine. "Gay People in Recovery." unpublished.

A one page paper highlighting the need to help homosexuals become integrated into the treatment community.

452 Noble, Elaine and Gerald Shulman. "Is the Population that is More Likely to Need Treatment less Likely to Get It?" unpublished.

This short paper addresses the issue of why lesbians are not getting the treatment they need.

453 ---. "How Do You Teach Acceptance to the Unaccepted?" Unpublished.

A one paper paper that argues that "treatment staff must be available and accepting to gay and lesbian chemically dependent people and their significant others."

454 Norris, John L. "Our Primary Purpose and the Special Purpose Group." Box 1980 ["The Grapevine"] October 1977: 6-9.

Norris discusses the concept of special purpose groups in AA. Among the groups he mentions are those serving the needs of homosexuals.

455 North, Dorthy B. "Skid Row Women." Women Who Drink. Ed. Vasanti Burtle. Springfield: Charles C. Thomas, 1979. 81-97.

Of the 20 respondants North used in her sample, seven were lesbians.

456 Nussbaum, L. "Program Helps Lesbian Alcoholics." Gay Community News 10 February 1979: 12.

Nussbaum explores the problems encountered by lesbian alcoholics and the Women's Alcoholism Program in Cambridge, MA.

457 O'Donnell, Mary. "Alcoholism and Co-Alcoholism: There is a Solution." Women: A Journal of Liberation 7.3 (1981): 64-9.

The article is reprinted from Lesbian Health Matters! (published by the Santa Cruz Women's Health Center). The text covers such topics as why there are so many lesbian alcoholics, how to identify a drinking problem, the signs of alcoholism, co-alcoholism, and how a lesbian alcoholic can get help. O'Donnell stresses that both the alcoholic and co-alcoholic need help. References for further reading follow the article.

458 ---. "Alcoholism and Co-Alcoholism: There is a Solution." PLGTF Bulletin 3.9 (1981): 6-7+.

An excerpt from Mary O'Donnell, et al's Lesbian Health Matters.

459 O'Donnell, Mary, Val Loeffler, Kater Pollock, and Ziesel Saunders. Lesbian Health Matters! Santa Cruz: Santa Cruz Women's Health Center, 1979: 73-84.

The book includes Mary O'Donnell's "Alcoholism and Co-Alcoholism" and is available from Santa Cruz Women's Center, 250 Locust Street, Santa Cruz, 95060. This chapter was reprinted in Women. [see Mary O'Donnell]

460 Oliver, Margot. "Killing Us Softly." Out From Under. Ed. Jean Swallow. San Francisco: Spinsters, Ink, 1983: 138-46.

Oliver's thesis is that "social conditioning may cause addiction, but the only way to cure it is to stop using."

461 Olmstead, Rose Ann. "Lesbians and Alcoholism." Thesis. Smith College School of Social Work, 1986.

The thesis identified what variables, in the experience of lesbians with alcoholism, contributed to the development of our enhanced vulnerability to alcoholism. Also, variables that were helpful and harmful to recovery were also identified.

462 O'Loughlin, Ray. "S[an] F[rancisco] Supervisors Take Antipopper Stand." Advocate 24 January 1984: 10.

Based on a December 5, 1983 decision of the San Francisco Board of Supervisors to ban the sale of alkyl nitrites to minors, the article discusses some potential health problems if poppers are inhaled.

463 "One Size Fits All." Box 1980. ["The Grapevine"] 39.3 (1982): 35.

We can infer that the anonymous author of this letter is a black lesbian. She argues that the AA program works because alcoholics' similarities are greater than their differences. She concludes: "I am not a gay alcoholic or a black alcoholic or a female alcoholic. I am just an alcoholic."

464 "The Only Requirement..." Box 1980 ["The Grapevine"] May 1975: 17.

The author, a lesbian, focuses her remarks on AA's Third Tradition: "The only requirement for AA membership is a desire to stop drinking."

465 "Outreach to Women: Including Bilingual/Bicultural Techniques." Los Angeles: Alcoholism Center for Women, 1983.

"Lesbians of any age--particularly those coming out" is listed as a major life crisis.

466 Oxford, Gerry. "It Can't Cure an Alcoholic." Body Politic 87 (1982): 35.

The article is a positive review of Vincent Virga's A Comfortable Corner.

467 P. Eric. "Living Sober: A Gay Man's Story." Village Voice 23 July 1985.

A 28 year old man with four year's sobriety tells his story.

468 P., Malinda. "Malinda P." A Woman Like You. Ed. Rachel V. San Francisco: Harper and Row, 1985. 64-75.

A lesbian recounts her experience of sobering up in AA.

469 Padric. "My Name is Padric and I'm and Alcoholic (gay)." Do You Think You're Different? New York: Alcoholics Anonymous, 1976. 9-10.

Padric stresses that AA's program of recovery is open to anyone who has the desire to stop drinking. Homosexuality is not the issue.

470 Parker, Frederick B. "Comparison of the Sex Temperment of Alcoholics and Moderate Drinkers." American Sociological Review 24 (1959): 366-74.

In this essay, "the role of deficient masculinity and/or latent homosexuality in the etiology of alcoholism is discussed within the framework of role and self theory."

471 ---. "Sex-Role Adjustment in Women Alcoholics." Quarterly Journal of Studies on Alcohol 33 (1972): 647-57.

The summary with the article reads: "Femininity of role-relevant preferences was lower, while emotionality was higher, in women alcoholics than in women moderate drinkers matched in age and education." Lesbianism is suggested by the author in his use of the term "deviant feminism."

472 Parkland, O. "Alkoholismi ja Homoseksualism." [Homosexuality and Alcoholism] Alkoholipolitiikkaa 4 (1957): 119-24.

The article is summarized in the Quarterly Journal of Studies on Alcohol 19 (1958): 519-20.

473 ---. "Alkoholismi ouch Hokusexualitet." [Homosexuality and Alcoholism] Alkoholipolitiikkaa 3 (1957): 75-80+.

The article is summarized in the Quarterly Journal of Studies on Alcohol 19 (1958): 519-20.

474 ---. "Alcoholism and Homosexuality." Quarterly Journal of Studies on Alcohol 19 (1958): 519-20.

A summary of Parkland's "Alkoholism och Homosexualitet" and "Alkoholismi ja Homoseksualism." Parkland found that both homosexuality and alcoholism are means to escape from manliness.

475 Patrick. "Je m'appelle Patrick, et je suis un alcoolique (homosexuel)." Vous croyez-vous Différent? trans. Service de la littérature AA du Québec. Montreal: Service de la Litérature du Québec, 1979.

Translation of Padric, "My Name is Padric and I'm an Alcoholic (gay)."

476 Patrick, Robert. "T-Shirts." Gay Plays. Ed. W.M. Hoffman. New York: Avon, 1979.

A realistic portrayal of alcoholism serves as a major theme in this play.

477 Peteros, Karen and Fran Miller. "Lesbian Health in a Straight World." Second Opinion: Coalition for the Medical Rights of Women (April 1982): 1-2+.

A discussion of alcoholism is included under a section on "The Mental Health of Lesbians." Concerns are raised over the inappropriate care lesbians receive in treatment; "care" that perpetuates alcoholism and drug abuse.

478 Phillips, S. "Gay AA's Multiply." Advocate 9 June 1971: 12.

The article is cited in The Alternative Press Index 3.2 (1971): 3.

479 Piasecki, Patricia. "The Day After Tomorrow Show." Out From Under. Ed. Jean Swallow. San Francisco: Spinsters, Ink, 1983: 199-203.

Piasecki's story is told in the form of a question/answer script for a TV show. She discusses her need for sobriety and how she sobered-up. Also, she effectively answers the question: "Why are you drinking soda with dinner instead of your usual wine."

480 "P[ennsylvani]a Council Hears Gay Needs." Gay Community News 14 April 1979: 7.

News article discussing Tom Ziebold and Ken William's testimony to the Pennsylvania Governor's Council on Drug and Alcohol Abuse. They urged the council to recognize "the special problems of gay persons seeking health care in facing cultural rejection, fearing disclosure of sexual and affectional feelings, and developing a comfortable sexual identity." They also pointed out that gay people, unlike any other social minority, often lack family support in recovery from a serious illness such as alcoholism.

481 Perdue, Lewis. "New Brew for Gays Makes Novel Debut." Advocate 29 May 1984: 20.

The article focuses on the development of Wilde's beer, manufactured for and marketed in the gay community. The ads for the beer are explicitly gay and romantic.

482 "Playboy Interview: Timothy Leary." Playboy 13.9 (1966): 93+.

In answering the question of whether LSD "can trigger the acting out of latent homosexual impulses" as had been reported, Leary responds: "On the contrary, the fact is that LSD is a specific cure for homosexuality." Both gay and lesbian examples are cited to support his claim.

483 Pohl, Melvin. "Medical Aspects of Cocaine Use." NAGAP Newsletter 5.3 (1984): 8.

A brief description of the medical aspects of cocaine. There is no specific mention of homosexuality.

484 ---. "Protracted Alcohol Abstinence Syndrome." NAGAP Newsletter 4.4 (1983): 2.

A general discussion of protracted alcohol abstinence syndrome without specific mention of homosexuality.

485 Polo, Carol A. "Common Sense Approach to Working with Gay Alcoholics." Alcohol and Drug Problems Association Convention, New Orleans, 1976.

The paper is cited in Gary A. MacPherson's "Homophobia of the Gay Alcoholic as a Factor for Consideration in the Treatment of Alcoholism."

486 "Poppers: Major AIDS Risk Factor." Out Front 10.9 (1985).

The article highlights research that concludes that: "Poppers are hazardous to the health and many be an important co-factor in causing AIDS."

487 "Position Paper on Gays and Alcoholism." NAGAP Newsletter 2.1 (1980): 2.

Summary of a statement delivered by Ginny Apuzzo concerning alcoholism in the lesbian/gay community.

488 Potter, Jesse. "Women and Sex--It's Enough to Drive Them to Drink." Women Who Drink. Ed. Vasanti Burtle. Springfield: Charles C. Thomas, 1979. 49-80.

Potter writes that although homosexuality "has also been ascribed to the woman drinker, based on her role in folklore as well as on some psychoanalytic thinking....it is clear there is not necessarily any correlation between alcoholism and lesbianism."

489 Powell, David J. Alcoholism and Sexual Dysfunction: Issues in Clinical Management. New York: Haworth Press, 1984.

Originally published as Volume 1, issue 3 of the Alcoholism Treatment Quarterly, this book includes Rebert W. Fuller's "Assessment of Sexual Functioning" and Dana Finnegan and David Cook's "Special Issues Affecting the Treatment of [Gay] Male and Lesbian Alcoholics."

490 ---. Preface. Alcoholism and Sexual Dysfunction. New York: Haworth Press, 1984. xiii-xvi.

In setting Dana Finnegan and David Cook's "Special Issues Affecting the Treatment of [Gay] Male and Lesbian Alcoholics," Powell comments that: "Ego distonic homosexuality is a significant issue to be addressed in alcoholism therapy." This issue is not, however, the basis of the Finnegan/Cook article.

491 "Prevention Strategies." California Alcoholism Review, January/February 1975, March/April 1975.

Prevention in the homosexuality community is discussed.

492 "The Pride Institute: An Interview with Elaine Noble." The Gay News-Telegraph 5.8 (1986): 13.

Noble discusses the founding of Pride Institute, the first residential treatment center designed around the needs of lesbians and gay men.

493 "Process of the Cells Learning to Function Together Again: An Interview with Karen Pruitt." Out From Under Ed. Jean Swallow. San Francisco: Spinsters, Ink, 1983. 65-70.

Pruitt, "a registered nurse at...[a] women's residential rehabilitation program," focuses her comments on the physiological aspects of alcohol addiction and withdrawal.

494 "Program Profile: The Whitman Walker Clinic, Inc." Alcoholism Education and Training News 2.6 (1979): 9.

The Gay Council on Drinking Behavior is mentioned.

495 Quaranta, J.V. "Alcoholism: A Study of Emotional Maturity and Homosexuality as Related Factors in Compulsive Drinking." Thesis. Fordham University, 1947.

The title is self explanatory.

496 R., G. "Without that Bond." Box 1980 ["The Grapevine"] 40.7 (1983): 38.

G.R.'s letter is written in response to a letter written by a lesbian concerning an article he had published in Box 1980. The author comments that "what she and I have in common is our alcoholism, and I'm happy about that--because without that bond to draw us together, she and I would never have reached out and touched one another."

497 R., Steve. "The All American Boy from Wyoming..." RFD 28 (1981): 37.

Steve's story focuses on his self hatred and guilt that resulted from his homosexuality and his homosexual activity. However, "With the help of others [in AA] I have come to accept my homosexuality and look upon it as a gift and an opportunity."

498 Ralston, Allen and Dawn VanDerzee. Issues of the Gay and Lesbian Populations in Ohio. Report Submitted to the Ohio Recovery Council Oversight Committee for Special Needs Populations, 28 June 1984.

The report points out the needs and issues of the homosexual community in relationship to alcoholism. It also makes suggestions as to how to reduce alcoholism in the Ohio homosexual community.

499 Ramée, F. and P. Michaux. "De Quelques Aspects de la Délinquance Sexuelle dans un Départment de l'ouest de la France." [Some Aspects of Sexual Offenses in a Province in Western France] Archive Belges de Médecine, Social Hygiene, Médecine du Travail and Médicine Legal 19 (1966): 79-85.

Homosexuality and alcoholism are discussed.

500 Ramos, Michael. Letter. "Alcohol." The Gay News-Telegraph 5.8 (1986): 10.

Ramos suggests that signs warning of the dangers of alcoholism be placed in bars.

501 Rathod, N.H., E. Gregory, and D. Blows. "Two-year Follow-up Study of Alcoholic Patients." British Journal of Psychiatry 112 (1966): 683-92.

In this study, "all the patients who gave a history of repeated homosexual practice relapsed."

502 Ray. "It has been Worth Living..." RFD 28 (1981): 33.

After telling about several "geographic cures" he took for his alcoholism, Ray tells how how he finally stopped drinking when he began going to AA with his then lover. Although the lover did not stay sober, Ray writes that: "I personally have found answers in AA."

503 Read, C.S. "The Psycho-pathology of Alcoholism and Some So-called Alcoholic Psychoses." Journal of Medical Science 66 (1920): 233-44.

Homosexuality is cited as a factor in alcoholism.

504 Read, Kenneth. Other Voices: The Style of a Male Homosexual Tavern. Novato, CA: Chandler and Sharp, 1980.

Read presents an anthropological analysis of a gay bar.

505 Reed, David. "The Multimillion-Dollar Mystery High." Christopher Street 3.7 (1979): 21-6+.

The debate over the health concerns of poppers is explained. Court cases concerning government attempts to regulate nitrites are cited as is the feud between "Rush" and "Pacific Ocean."

506 Reality Finally Dawns: The Story of Gay Alcoholism. RFD 28 (1981).

This is a special issue of RFD which includes "Alcoholism: Symptoms of Progress," "Alcoholism in Our Community," Kevin Cox's "Review," Ron F.'s "We Met That Evening and He Told Me How He Stayed Sober", Dick H.'s "Alcoholism Took Him Places Most of Us Would Never See," Doug H.'s "I Grew Up Alcoholic and Gay in a Small Southern Town," John's "I Had Become a Co-Alcoholic," "Lovers and Other Co-Alcoholics," Andy M.'s "The Joy of Living," Susan M.'s "Living With and Alcoholic," John Michael's "The Gay Drinking Problem," Steve R.'s "The All American Boy from Wyoming," Ray's "It's Been Worth Living," Larry V.'s Glamor Queen from the Mid-West," and Thomas Zeibold's "Alcoholism is an Illness."

507 "Recovery is Power in the Now: An Interview with Suzanne Balcer." _Out From Under_. Ed. Jean Swallow. San Francisco: Spinsters, Ink, 1983. 79-83.

"Balcer is the Coordinator of Women's Services at the only totally gay and lesbian alcoholism center in this country." Her comments focus on recovery programs.

508 Reitzell, Jean Manneim. "A Comparative Study of Hysterics, Homosexuals, and Alcoholics Using Content Analysis of Rorschach Responses." Thesis. Clairmont Graduate School, 1949.

The thesis was summarized for an article of the same title which appeared in the _Rorschach Research Exchange_.

509 ---. "A Comparative Study of Hysterics, Homosexuals, and Alcoholics Using Content Analysis of Rorschauch Responses." _Rorschach Research Exchange_ 13.1 (1949): 127-41.

Reitzell's thesis is "that alcoholics, whose behavior becomes obvious later than hysteric or homosexual behavior would be the least likely to show a definite Rorschach pattern."

510 "Report Released on Lesbian/Gay Substance Abuse." _Plexus_ 11.5 (1984): 4.

A summary of _Substance Abuse: Patterns and Barriers to Treatment for Gay Men and Lesbians in San Francisco_.

511 Riess, Bernard F. and Jeanne M. Safer. "Homosexuality in Females and Males." _Gender and Disordered Behavior_. Eds. Edith Gomberg and Violet Franks. New York: Brunner/Mazel, 1979.

Alcoholism is one of the pathological categories mentioned.

512 Riggall, Robert M. "Homosexuality and Alcoholism." Psychoanalysis and Psychoanalytic Review 10 (1923): 157-69.

Riggall equates craving for sweets, alcohol, or tobacco with fellatio which "has obvious unconscious reference to the mother's nipple, and is only another proof of the large part a mother-fixation can play both in homosexuality and alcoholism."

513 Riley, Kathy. "Is It Personal Preference or Integrity." Big Mama Rag 7.11 (1979): 15.

Riley explains the "little suicides," those dependencies which can easily be ignored if they aren't obviously destructive. Smoking, drinking, and eating meat are used as examples. LUNA, Lesbians United to "Nip" Alcoholism, is mentioned.

514 Robe, Lucy Barry. "Gay AA Groups Help More, Lesbians Suggest." The Journal 1 August 1980: 10.

The article focuses on some of the findings of LeClair Bissell's research with lesbian AA members.

515 Rofes, Eric. "An End to the Silence About Suicide: A Gay Issue that Cannot be Ignored." Advocate 9 August 1979: 15-9.

In a section on alcoholism, Rofes writes: "For many recovering alcoholics, the struggle is difficult and can become overwhelming. If success in fighting alcoholism seems remote, some people choose to kill themselves rather than continue the fight."

516 ---. "I Thought People Like That Killed Themselves": Lesbians, Gay Men and Suicide. San Francisco: Grey Fox, 1983.

Of particular interest is the chapter "Substance Abuse and Gay Suicide" which begins: "Substance abuse has consistently been linked to increased risk of suicide in the general population. Counselors who work at suicide prevention agencies report a strong correlation between suicide attempts and alcohol and drug abuse among the lesbian and gay male population." Rofes then discusses the aspects of chemical addiction and suicide before encouraging: "The lesbian and gay community must also address the issue of alcoholism as it looks at the role suicide plays in our community."

517 Room, Robin. "AIDS and Alcohol: Epidemiological and Behavioral Aspects." NIAAA Consultation on AIDS and Alcohol, 4-5 November 1985.

Room found that gay and bisexual men were very aware that they were more prone to practice unsafe sex while using alcohol or other drugs. The same degree of awareness was not as clear among IV drug users, hemophiliacs, and other HTLV-III positive individuals and their partners.

518 Ross, B. "Alcoholism and Lesbians...Brown Bag..." Big Mama Rag 11.7 (1983): 4.

The article is cited in The Alternative Press Index 15.3 (1983): 3.

519 Rubin, Isadore. The "Third Sex." New York: New Book, 1961.

Includes Charles Allen's article, "The Aging Homosexual."

520 Rudy, David R. Becoming Alcoholic: Alcoholics Anonymous and the Reality of Alcoholism. Carbondale: Southern Illinois University Press, 1986.

A gay man Rudy encountered commented that he first came to AA "to figure himself out." The man's experiences are not elaborated upon.

521 Ryan, Caitlin C. Letter. "NL/GHEF." [National Lesbian/Gay Health Education Foundation]. NALGAP Newsletter 6.1 (1984): 4.

Ryan explains and requests help for a survey currently being conducted on lesbian health needs.

522 Ryan, Jack. "AIDS." NALGAP Newsletter 7.2 (1986): 2-3.

Ryan summarizes various papers and booklets concerning AIDS and chemical dependency.

523 ---. "Alcoholism and Sexuality: Some Notes for Counselors." unpublished manuscript.

A manuscript that was distributed while giving his paper on "The Sexual (Re)Adjustment of the Alcoholic."

524 ---. "Booze in the Gay World." High Gear April 1978: 15.

Ryan's thesis is that for the 10% of the population who are alcoholic: "It's never too late [to stop drinking] as long as you are alive."

525 [---]. Editorial. NALGAP Newsletter 6.3 (1985): 2-3.

Written on April Fools Day, Ryan reflects on the "divine foolishness that motivates us all." Mention is made of what it used to be like when he was drinking and what it is like for him today.

526 ---. Editorial. NALGAP Newsletter 7.2 (1986): 1-2.

In part, Ryan mentions how drinking and drugging affect the immune system.

527 [---]. "Grants-Funding: What's to be Done." NAGAP Newsletter 5.1 (1983): 3-4.

A general overview of grant writing with special emphasis on lesbian/gay concerns.

528 ---. Letter. "NALGAP Praises Drug Abuse Article." _The Works_ 5.5 (1986): 7.

A brief letter which focuses on the National Association of Lesbian and Gay Alcoholism Professionals.

529 ---. "The Need for Regional Chapters." _NALGAP Newsletter_ 6.1 (1984): 1-2.

Ryan discusses the beginning of the National Association of Lesbian and Gay Alcoholism Professionals' mid-west regional chapter and the need for such networking among substance abuse professionals.

530 ---. "The Sexual (Re)Adjustment of the Alcoholic." National Congress on Alcohol and Drug Problems, San Francisco, 16 December 1974.

In this workshop, Ryan explains that: "In the case of the alcoholic who has become involved in homosexual activities during his drinking days, we [therapists] may very well be called upon to assist him in establishing his sexual identity." A manuscript titled "Alcoholism and Sexuality--Some Notes for Counselors" was distributed at this seminar.

531 S., K. "Exclusive--or More Inclusive?" _Box 1980_ ["The Grapevine"] October 1977: 11-3.

In this discussion of the role of special purpose groups in AA, S.K. cites homosexual groups as one example.

532 S., W. "The Many Masks of Alcohol." _Box 1980_ ["The Grapevine"] 40.7 (1983): 9-10.

W.S. lists some of the ways alcohol disguises itself into deluded thinking. Disguise 11 is that "AA won't work for me because I'm young/old/gay/straight/white/black/red/yellow/Catholic..."

533 Sabatini, Raphael. Rev. of Queer. By William S. Burroughs. RFD 47 (1986): 61.

Sabatubu mentions that the book is a "drugged chronicle" of a gay man.

534 Saergert, Linda. "Homosexuality in the Workplace." Fourteenth ALMACA Conference, Boston, 14 November 1985.

Saergert writes that: "For the chemically dependent homosexual in recovery, there is the added burden of being forced to meet in gay and lesbian bars for acceptance, where drugs and alcohol are readily available.

535 Sage, Wayne. "Inside the Colossal Closet." Human Behavior (August 1975): 16-23.

A good discussion of the cultural implications that bars play in the gay community. A dominant theme is the question of whether gay bars are simply a bigger closet.

536 Saghir, Marcel T. and Eli Robins. Male and Female Homosexuality: A Comprehensive Investigation. Baltimore: Williams and Wilkins, 1973.

The book includes statistical information on alcohol and non-prescriptive drug use for both lesbians and gay men.

537 Saghir, Marcel T., et al. "Homosexuality: III. Psychiatric Disorders and Disability in the Male Homosexual." American Journal of Psychiatry 126 (1970): 1079-86.

The article includes a brief section on "Alcohol Consumption or Related Problems."

538 ---. "Homosexuality. IV. Psychiatric Disorders and Disability in the Female Homosexual." American Journal of Psychiatry 127 (1970): 147-54.

The abstract for the article reads: "A study of 57 homosexual women and 43 single heterosexual controls revealed slightly more clinical significant changes and disability in the lives of the homosexual women as compared with the heterosexual women. The chief differences were in increased prevalence of alcoholism and attempted suicide.

539 "Sailor's Return." The Way Back. 1981. Washington, D.C.: Whitman-Walker Clinic, 1982. 41f.

The focus of this gay man's story is his many geographic cures before joining AA.

540 Samson, Stacy. "Talented, Dry Dykes." Bay Windows 25-30 May 1985: 23.

A review of Boston's Amethyst Women's annual talent show. The beginning of the review discusses the importance of chem-free space.

541 San Francisco AIDS Foundation. Alcohol, Drugs, and Your Health. San Francisco: San Francisco AIDS Foundation, 1984.

Because "Recent research has indicated that alcohol, as well as such street drugs as amphetamines (speed), marijuana, and nitrite inhalants (poppers), all damage the immune system, leaving the user open to infection and cancer," this pamphlet explains how alcohol and other drugs are related to AIDS. Suggestions are given for people who use alcohol and drugs and fear they might have AIDS.

542 ---. Designing An Effective AIDS Prevention Campaign Strategy for San Francisco: Results from the Second Probability Sample of an Urban Gay Male Community San Francisco: San Francisco AIDS Foundation, 1985.

The study found that inebriation ("enough so that you would not want to drive a car") while engaging in sex was present in 18% of the 500 gay men surveyed. The report goes on to say that there is a high correlation between drinking and unsafe sex practices. Added to these factors is the denial among gay men about the possible dangers of alcohol and drug use/abuse and the links with AIDS.

543 Sandmaier, Marian. "Alcohol, Mood Altering Drugs, and Smoking." The New Our Bodies Ourselves: A Book By and For Women. Ed. The Boston Women's Health Collective. New York: Simon and Schuster, 1984: 33-40.

Although lesbianism is not specifically addressed in the essay, resources for the lesbian community are included in the bibliography which follows the article.

544 ---. The Invisible Alcoholics: Women and Alcohol Abuse in America. New York: McGraw Hill, 1980.

In her chapter on lesbianism, Sandmaier writes that "If she drinks at all, the lesbian stands a good chance of developing an alcohol problem." Statistical information is provided as well as personal experiences.

545 Sargent, Lee. Twilight Passion. San Diego: Phenix, 1969.

An "autobiographical" novel depicting a lesbian's struggle with alcoholism. Very compassionately written even though it is packaged as a trashy novel.

456 Sappell, Jan. "Alcoholism Center: 'Love Keeps Me Here.'" Lesbian Tide 5.4 (1976): 26+.

An overview of the program offered by Los Angeles' Women and Alcoholism Center. Focus is on both staff and patients. The article ends with the comment that "Alcoholism is the disease that has brought them together and together they are working their way toward a new and better life."

547 Saunders, Edward J. "Homosexual Recovering Alcoholics: A Descriptive Study." Alcohol World 8.2 (1983/84): 18-22.

A good overview of previous studies on homosexuality and alcoholism.

548 Scenitz, W.C. and J.M. Swanson, eds. From Grounded Theory to Clinical Practice. Menlo Park, CA: Addison-Wesley, 1986.

This book includes Robert J. Kus' "From Grounded Theory to Clinical Practice."

549 Schaffer, Perrin. "Gay Alcoholics Reveal Life Styles and Attitudes." Gay 21 August 1972: 1+.

We have been unable to locate a copy of this article and we no longer know our source for it.

550 Schaefer, Susan and S. Evans. "Women's Sexuality and Alcoholism." International Conference on Alcoholism, Oxford, England, April 1982.

The paper is cited in Sharon Wilsnack's "Drinking, Sexuality, and Sexual Dysfunction in Women."

551 ---. "Affectional Preference and Chemical Dependency: Treatment Considerations." Conference on Chemical Abuse and Sexuality: Defining Relationships, University of Minnesota, Minneapolis, September 1980.

The paper is cited in Sharon Wilsnack's "Drinking, Sexuality, and Sexual Dysfunction in Women."

552 Schechter, Phyl. "Dealing with Life Sober." Big Mama Rag 7.11 (1979): 10.

Schechter relates how turning to friends in LUNA, Lesbians United to "Nip" Alcoholism, helped her deal with a frustrating experience without drinking.

553 Schietinger, H. "Lesbian Health." Medical Self-Care 21 (1983): 53.

Schietinger argues that the stress in being homosexual is a major factor in the high rate of alcoholism in the lesbian community.

554 Schilder, Paul. "The Psychogenesis of Alcoholism." Quarterly Journal of Studies on Alcoholism 2 (1941): 277-92.

Schilder, in his discussion of alcoholic hallucinations, claims "that human beings choose for addiction drugs which physiologically will increase tendencies previously present. Homosexuality can be almost experimentally produced by cocaine intoxication which in turn is mostly resorted to by those with latent homosexual cravings."

555 Schoenberg, S., S. Goldberg, and D.A. Shore, eds. Homosexuality and Social Work . New York: Haworth Press, 1984.

Includes M.A. Zehner and J. Lewis' "Homosexuality and Alcoholism: Social Developmental Perspectives."

556 Schoener, Gary. "The Heterosexual Norm in Chemical Dependency Treatment Programs: Some Personal Observations." STASH Capsules 8.1 (1976): 1-2.

An explanation of the types of homophobia found in treatment centers is given.

557 Schultz, Ardelle. "Radical Feminism: A Treatment Modality for Addicted Women." Development in the Field

<u>of Drug Abuse</u>. Ed. Edward Senay, et al. Cambridge: Shankman Publishing, 1974.

In a section titled "The Problems of Women Who are Lesbian," Schultz cites examples of homophobia within a treatment community and the negative impact it has on lesbians in recovery. She concludes this section explaining that "the needs of the Lesbian woman for a sense of self/worth, for self/confidence, and self/direction, are much the same as other women with addiction problems."

558 Schwartz, Linda. <u>Alcoholism Among Lesbians/Gay Men: A Critical Problem in Critical Proportions</u>. Phoenix: Do It Now Foundation, 1980.

Schwartz explains the new awareness both within the homosexual and treatment communities concerning alcoholism among lesbians and gay men. A special focus is on ways in which treatment professionals can educate themselves. It also includes Meg Christian's story of addiction and recovery.

559 ---. <u>Alcoholism in the Lesbian/Gay Community: Coming to Terms with an Epidemic</u>. Phoenix: Do It Now Foundation, 1980.

Originally titled "Gay Men and Lesbians and Alcoholism: Coming to Terms with an Epidemic," this pamphlet begins by giving an overview of the alcohol problem in the homosexual community. This section is followed by an explanation of how the alcoholic homosexual can get help. The final section explains the increased awareness of alcoholism that has come about in the past few years.

560 ---. "Gay Alcoholism: Epidemic Meets with Hostility from Treatment Workers." <u>Drug Survival News</u> 8.6 (1980): 8-10.

Schwartz gives a good overview of the problem of alcoholism in the homosexual community by citing many studies. But, full citations for her references are not given. There is also a lengthy discussion of NAGAP and what can be done to overcome homophobia among treatment professionals.

561 Scott, Edward M. "Psychosexuality of the Alcoholic." Psychological Reports 4.4 (1958): 599-602.

Scott writes that he "is well aware that some alcoholics are homosexual. But, to conclude that this is 'basic' is to conclude too much." He concludes that: "Clinical studies of 300 consecutive case records of alcoholics suggest that the dominant psychosexual factor is that of immaturity. This suggestion stems from the high divorce rate, which is interpreted, on the quotations from patient's records, not as an indication of latent homosexuality, but rather as an inability to assume responsibility for one's state in life."

562 Selwyn, Peter A. "AIDS: What Is Now Known: II. Epidemiology." Hospital Practice 15 June 1986: 127-64.

Mention is made of poppers as a co-factor in AIDS.

563 "A Seminarians Story." The Way Back. 1981. Washington, D.C.: Whitman-Walker Clinic, 1982. 21f.

This gay man's drinking did not accelerate until after he left the seminary.

564 Senay, Edward, et al, eds. Development in the Field of Drug Abuse. Cambridge: Shankman Publishing, 1974.

The book includes Ardelle Schultz's "Radical Feminism."

565 "Sex a Factor in Treatment." Journal 8.7 (1979): 4.

William Crawford cites this article in his Homosexuality in Canada with the following annotation: "Not seen. Compiler cannot vouch for gay content."

566 "Shattered." Box 1980 ["The Grapevine"] 42.11 (April 1986): 29-30.

The author tells about how his life and sobriety was affected when he learned he had AIDS.

567 Shernoff, Michael. "So Many Drugs, So Little Time." New York Native 41 (1982): 12-13+.

Shernoff defines such terms as "recreational drugs," "drug abuse," and "drug dependency." He then explains the affects of drugs on an individual and what one can do if they think they have a drug problem.

568 ---. "When the Individual Isn't the Problem: Family Therapy for Lesbians and Gay Men." New York Native 15-28 August 1975: 28+.

One of the case studies Shernoff uses to explain the need for family therapy in dealing with gay/lesbian clients concerns an alcoholic lesbian.

569 Shilts, Randy. "Alcoholism: A Look in Depth at How a National Menace is Affecting the Gay Community." Advocate 25 February 1974: 16-19+.

Shilts discusses the social aspects of the gay bar, life for the gay alcoholic, co-alcoholism, treatment, and recovery. This is the first major study published in the gay press.

570 ---. "The Way Out: Stonewall Therapy." Advocate 30 June 1976: 23+.

Based on client and staff interviews, Shilts describes the treatment approach of the Stonewall Human Growth Center, an all gay alcohol/drug treatment facility in Seattle.

571 ---. "The President's Nephew." Christopher Street 3.11 (1979): 29-35.

The article is based on an interview with William Carter Spann, nephew of President Jimmy Carter. In it, Spann's chemical addiction and homosexual activity are addressed.

572 Shillin, Alana. "A Way to Fundraise That Works." _Out From Under_. Ed. Jean Swallow. San Francisco: Spinsters, Ink, 1983: 134-37.

Schillin's thesis is that it is possible to raise funds without alcohol.

573 Shoener, G. "The Heterosexual Norm in Chemical Dependency Treatment Programs: Some Personal Observations." _STASH Capsules_ 3.1 (January 1976).

Some observations on how homosexuals do not have their needs met in treatment.

574 Shulman, Jerry and Elain Noble. "Chemical Dependence, Co-Dependence, and the Gay and Lesbian Community." _ARCircular_ 3.1 (March 1986): 3f.

A discussion of problems lesbians and gay men face in receiving treatment for alcoholism and co-alcoholism. The article includes sections on "Societal Lack of Acceptance," "Treatment Resources Needed," and "The Gay Family System."

575 Siegel, Larry. "AIDS: It's Relationship to Alcohol and Other Drugs." _NALGAP Newsletter_ 7.2 (1986): 3-4.

In this article, Siegel defines AIDS, gives an overview of the medical issues, discusses the role of alcohol and other drugs in the development of AIDS, and the treatment of chemical dependency as a adjunct to the management of AIDS.

576 ---. "AIDS: Relationship to Alcohol and Other Drugs." _Journal of Substance Abuse Treatment_ 3.4 (1986): 271-4.

Siegel writes that: "The correlation between drug use and the development of AIDS in several populations [including homosexual men] is striking and it is suggested that definitive research into this possible co-factor be initiated urgently."

577 Siegel, L.T., et al. "Popping and Snorting Volatile Nitrites: A Current Fad for Getting High." American Journal of Pschiatry 135.10 (1978): 1216-18.

In a discussion of various nitrites, the authors comment that "Until recently male homosexuals indulged in these drugs more than other groups did."

578 "Silver and Sobriety." The Way Back. 1981. Washington, D.C.: Whitman-Walker Clinic, 1982. 15f.

An English expatriate now living in America tells her story of two marriages she had before realizing she was a lesbian and what AA means to her.

579 Silverstein, Charles and Edmund White. The Joy of Gay Sex. New York: Crown, 1977.

Written in dictionary form, the authors include a definition of alcoholism. Headings also include specific drugs and drugs are mentioned under descriptions of such sexual practices as "fist fucking."

580 Sisley, Emily L. and Bertha Harris. The Joy of Lesbian Sex. New York: Crown, 1977.

Written in dictionary form, the authors include definitions of alcoholism and drug abuse.

581 Small, Edward J. and Barry Leach. "Counseling Homosexual Alcoholics: Ten Case Histories." Journal of Studies on Alcohol 38 (1977): 2077-86.

The summary provided with the text reads: "The case histories of 10 male homosexual alcoholics are presented, and psychoanalytic theories about the link between homosexuality and alcoholism are reviewed." The authors state that: "The case sketches that follow suggest that homosexuality and alcoholism in men are probably independent states, and that homosexuality need not be an obstacle to therapy or recovery from alcoholism under certain conditions."

582 Smalldon, John L. "The Etiology of Chronic Alcoholism: A Resume of the Literature with Two Case Reports." Psychiatric Quarterly 4 (1933): 640-61.

Smalldon mentions Karl Abraham's theory that homosexuality is an underlying cause of alcoholism.

583 Smith, David E., et al. A Multicultural View of Drug Abuse: Proceedings of the National Drug Abuse Conference, 1977. Cambridge, Schenkman, 1970.

The book includes Tama Dawn Judd's "A Survey of Non-Gay Alcoholism Treatment Agencies and Services Offered for Gay Women and Men" and Louis Manqual's "Management Issues with Homosexuality in an Adolescent Drug Treatment Program."

584 ---. "PCP and Sexual Dysfunction." Journal of Psychedelic Drugs 12 (1980): 269-73.

One case involved a 20 year old, white, homosexual male.

585 Smith, Nina Jo. "Alcohol and Violence Against Us." Off Our Backs 12.8 (1982): 27.

"This article is written in hopes of expanding our definition of violence against women to include the violence we experience in our lives as a result of alcohol." Smith cites statistics which verify the harm alcohol does to women and lesbians, 35% of whom can be classified as alcoholic.

586 ---. "Alcoholism: Violence Against Lesbians." _Out From Under_. Ed. Jean Swallow. San Francisco: Spinsters, Ink, 1983: 129-33.

The article is a reprint of "Alcohol and Violence Against Us."

587 Smith, Stuart B. and Max A. Schneider. "Treatment of Gays in a Straight Environment: Gay Alcoholics, Drug Addicts Survive a 'Straight in-patient Milieu.'" National Drug Abuse Conference, Seattle, 3-8 April 1978.

Smith and Schneider write that: "Some critics feel that a heterosexual (straight) environment is not conducive for gays because of their unique problems, life style and lack of knowledge and understanding on the part of the heterosexual staff members....This paper addresses these issues and indicates that gays can survive and thrive in a straight in-patient treatment milieu."

588 Smith, Thomas M. _AIDS and Alcoholism: Denial Strikes Again_ San Francisco: San Francisco Department of Public Health, 1985.

Smith mentions the IV drug use/AIDS connection while arguing that denial of the alcohol/AIDS connection is rampant. He demonstrates that the alcohol/AIDS factor is greater than the understanding that drunkeness can lead to unsafe-sex.

589 ---. "AIDS and Substance Abuse Counseling with Gay Men." San Francisco: by the author, 1986.

"The high prevalence of both AIDS and substance abuse in urban gay male populations in the United States and the connections between AIDS and substance abuse (direct tranmission by needle sharing, immunosuppression effects of drugs and disinhibition leading to unsafe sexual practices) press upon counselors of gay men to become familiar with several counseling aspects of AIDS relationship to chemical dependency. Strategies for recovery should be client centered, supportive, sex positive and non homophobic, focusing on all levels of biopsychological and existential functioning. The following areas are deliniated: AIDS/substance abuse information, compounding psychosocial factors, physical health counseling, sexuality counseling, counseling substance abusers who have AIDS or ARC, HTLV III antibody test counseling, couples counseling and community approach."

590 ---. "Alcohol and AIDS: Information Needs of the At Risk and General Population." San Francisco General Hospital, San Francisco, 4 November 1985.

A section of the paper is devoted to issues relating to gay and bi-sexual men.

591 ---. Alcohol. Immunity. San Francisco: San Francisco General Hospital, nd.

The thesis of this pamphlet is that "Alcohol certainly is not the cause of AIDS. However, excessive alcohol can weaken the immune system in a variety of ways." Those ways are discussed.

592 ---. "Factors Involved in Individualizing Strategic Psychotherapy and Holistic Approaches to the Treatment of Gay Male Alcohol Abusers." unpublished manuscript.

Brief case material is presented describing how various factors (e.g. values, life stages, "coming out" process) are utilized to individualize treatment for gay male alcohol abusers.

593 ---. Letter. "No Mass Hysteria Here." New York Native 16-29 August 1982.

Smith cites statistics that show that alcoholism is higher in the homosexual community than in the non-gay population. The letter was written in response to "Creative Sex, Creative Medicine."

594 ---. "New Thoughts About an Old Problem: Gay Brains and Booze." San Francisco: Department of Public Health, 1983.

Smith focuses on how alcohol abuse damages brain cells. He suggests that "The negative symptoms of brain injury in the lesbian/gay alcoholic (lack of responsibility taking, depression, rudeness) may be erroneously attributed to the individual's homosexuality."

595 ---. "Specific Approaches and Techniques in the Treatment of Gay Male Alcohol Abusers." Journal of Homosexuality 7.4 (1982): 53-70.

"An extended discussion of specific therapeutic approaches and techniques with homosexual male alcohol abusers, including dealing with low self-esteem, sober sex, getting high, getting 'far out' sexually, double lives, second rate relationships, social bonding, and aging."

596 "Something was Missing." The Way Back. 1981. Washington, D.C.: Whitman-Walker Clinic, 1982. 75-82.

This man's story of addiction and recovery through AA mentions his interest in leather bars.

597 Sonnabend, Joseph, Steven S. Witkin, and David T. Purtillo. "Acquired Immunodeficiency Syndrome, Opportunistic Infections, and Malignancies in Male Homosexuals: A Hypothesis of Etiologic Factors in Pathogenesis." Journal of the American Medical Association 6 May 1983: 2370.

The authors identify recreational drug use as a possible co-factor in AIDS.

598 "Special Problems with Alcoholism in the Gay and Lesbian Community were Discussed by Top NIAA Staffers with Representatives of the National Assn. of Gay

Alcoholism Professionals (NAGAP) and Others at a July 14 Meeting." The Alcoholism Report 8.19 (1980): 6.

The title is self explanatory.

599 Stall, Ron, et al. "Alcohol and Drug Use During Sexual Activity and Compliance with Safe Sex Guidelines for AIDS: The AIDS Behavioral Research Project." unpublished manuscript.

The paper describes the association between drug and alcohol use during sexual activity and high risk sex for AIDS. The authors found a strong relationship between drug/alcohol use during sex and non-compliance with safe sex techniques.

600 Stephens, Bryan. "Alcoholism: The Dark Side of Gay." The Magazine of the Texas Commission on Alcoholism 6.3 (1980): 7-10.

Stephens writes that "the gay lifestyle supports chemical use. A great deal of our lifestyle is centered around alcohol and drug environments. When a person first comes out and is introduced to a chemical environment--whether it be a bar, bookstore or bath--he develops a pattern of chemical use with his sexuality and doesn't deal with self-acceptance and fear." The pattern is discussed in detail.

601 Sterne, Muriel W. and David J. Pittman. Drinking Patterns in the Ghetto. St. Louis: Social Science Institute, Washington University, 1972.

This study of drinking habits among blacks showed that 36% of the lesbians living in the project were either heavy or problem drinkers. (vol. 2, p. 585)

602 Stewart, Samuel M. "To a Young, Gay Alcoholic." Advocate 8 July 1982: 35-38.

An open letter by a man who has been sober since 1947.

A personal, non-statistical discussion of the problem of alcoholism and a process of recovery is given.

603 Stonekey, Sharon. "Reminders." Out From Under. Ed. Jean Swallow. San Francisco: Spinsters, Ink, 1983: 46-9.

Stonekey gives a good, subtle overview of AA and how homophobia can exclude people from the program.

604 [Stowe, Perry]. Secret in a Bottle. New York: Pagent, 1952.

Published pseudonymously under the name Flint Holland. [see Flint Holland]

605 Strecker, E. One Man's Meat. New York: Macmillan, 1949.

Strecker writes that "our experience does not justify any sweeping statement concerning a basic homosexual trend in the alcoholic."

606 "Streets, Jail, the Mental Ward." The Way Back. 1981. Washington, D.C.: Whitman-Walker, Clinic, 1982. 29f.

A lesbian tells her story of alcohol addiction and recovery through AA.

607 "Substance Abuse in the Gay/Lesbian Community." Gaylife 11.11 (September 12, 1985): 7.

A general discussion of alcoholism in the gay/lesbian community based around a case study of a gay man.

608 Swallow, Jean. Out From Under: Sober Dykes and Our Friends. San Francisco: Spinsters, Ink, 1984.

In her introduction, Swallow states that 38% of all lesbians are alcoholic and 30% have a drinking problem. The first section of the book deals with the recovery process. Section two covers physical aspects of alcoholism. A section titled "The Politics of Our Addictions" emphasizes that alcoholism is a cultural problem. [see Claudia Kraehe's "Breath of a Gorilla Girl," Suzanne Hendrich's "On My Two Year Birthday," A.'s "Fall Journal," Mary Wheelan's "The Line," Faith's "Four," Kitty Tsui's "In Training," Sim Kallan's "1973 I Decided to Stop Shooting Dope," Sharon Stonekey's "Reminders," Meg Christian's "Turning It Over," Jean Swallow's "What is Calistoga?" "A Process of the Cells Learning to Function Again," "To Keep From Being Controlled," "Recovery is Power in the Now," "In Sobriety You Get Life," "It's a Wonder We Have Sex at All," "There is a Jewel in this Process," "Catherine Risiningflame Moirai's "Four Poems in Search of a Sober Reader," Abby Willowroot's "Creativity, Politics, and Sobriety," Nina Jo Smith's "Alcoholism: Violence Against Lesbians," Alana Schilling's "There is Another Way to Fundraise," Margot Oliver's "Killing Us Softly," Cathy Arnold's "This Kettle of Fish," Trish Larkin's "The Meaning of Rapture," Cathy Arnold's "Refrain," Alice Aldrich's "Sobering Thoughts," Red Arobateau's "Confessions of a Not-So-Ex Alcoholic," Karen Voltz's "Womenrest: Sometimes in Sobriety You Have to Make Changes," Judith McDaniel's "First Tries Don't Always Work, Chapter 5," Jean Swallow's "Recovery: The Story of an ACA," Patricia Piasecki's "The Day After Tomorrow Show," Marian Michener's "Three Glasses of Wine Have Been Removed From This Story," and Sherry Thomas' "The Sober Dyke."

609 ---. "Recovery: The Story of an ACA." <u>Out from Under</u>. Ed. Jean Swallow. San Francisco: Spinsters, Ink, 1983: 187-99.

Reflections of an adult child of an alcoholic.

610 ---. "The Rhododendrons." <u>Out From Under</u>. Ed. Jean Swallow. San Francisco: Spinsters, Ink, 1983: xii.

Swallow uses rhododendrons as a metaphor for life in a drug free community.

611 ---. "What is Calistoga?" Out from Under. Ed. Jean Swallow. San Francisco: Spinsters, Ink, 1983: 52-64.

Swallow's reflection focuses on her life today and memories of the past. She discusses "the way back," "courting," "the holidays," "friends," and "the way forward," before concluding "So the refrigerator is full of Calistoga, there is water in the kettle for tea. I am still healing, tearing out parts of myself like I was a garden of weeds, tearing out patches of cannibalism and drinking and replanting with new patience and the smell of old memories."

612 Swanson, D.W.; S.D. Loomis; R. Lukesh; R. Cronin; and J.A. Smith. "Clinical Features of the Female Homosexual Patient: A Comparison with the Heterosexual Patient." Journal of Nervous and Mental Disease 155 (1972): 119-24.

Lesbians exceeded heterosexual women in reported alcohol problems.

613 Szasz, Thomas S. The Manufacture of Madness. New York: Harper and Row, 1970.

Szasz links the parallel stigmas of homosexuality and alcoholism.

614 Norman. "To My Fellow Gay Christians and Dignitarians." Dignity/New Haven Newsletter December 1982.

After sharing his own struggle with alcoholism, Norman writes that "The Holiday season is simply an excuse because of social acceptability to overindulge and to drink and/or drug to excess. (Do you?) Practice moderation at ALL times, or if it be the case, recognize the problem and SEEK HELP!"

615 Tabori, J. "Homosexuality as Psychic Background of Alcoholism, Psychoanalysis of Cases." Psychiatric Praxia Psychoannal 3 (1933): 10-19.

Tabori claims that incompletely repressed homosexuality which the id is unable to sublimate causes alcoholism.

616 "A Tale of Two Couples." The Sentinel 3 April 1981.

An interview with two gay couples. In each couple, one man is alcoholic.

617 Tapper, Donna and Magnon Sauber. Human Services and the Gay and Lesbian Population of New York City: Emerging Services, Emerging Issues. New York: Community Council of Greater New York, 1986.

The focus in a section titled "Alcoholism and Substance Abuse Services" is on where gay/lesbian alcoholics can receive assistance in New York.

618 Tarras, Dave. "ACOA." NALGAP Newsletter 6.4 (1985): [4].

Tarras reports on what it was like to represent the National Association of Lesbian and Gay Alcoholism Professionals at the First National Convention of Adult Children of Alcoholics.

620 Taylor, Nancy. "Alcohol Abuse Prevention Among Women: A Community Approach." National Council on Alcoholism 1982 Annual Alcoholism Forum. Washington, D.C. April 1982.

Taylor's discussion focuses on "three non-mutually exclusive, ethically and economically diverse populations of women who may be identifed as showing the common feature of an alcoholic abuse rate of 30-60%": lesbians, adult daughters of alcoholics, and incest/battering survivors. She discusses the community-based approach for systematically "identifying and delivering prevention activities to adult women at high risk."

621 ---. "Making News With Alcohol Abuse Education: Inter-agency Networking for Media Outreach to Women and

Youth." Los Angeles: Alcoholism Center for Women, n.d.

"This paper explores the beneficial effects of inter-agency networking as part of systematic media outreach on the part of community and hospital based programs." One of the targeted populations discussed is lesbians.

622 Thanepohn, Susan G. "Homophobia, Counselor Reluctance Block Gay Treatment." The U.S. Journal of Drug and Alcohol Dependence 9.11 (1985): 22.

A discussion of "the [subtle] implications and ramifications of homophobic reactions in the treatment context." The article is based on an interview with Dana Finnegan and Emily McNally.

623 "Therapy Group Seeks to Assist Gay Alcoholics." Star-Ledger Newark, NJ 5 May 1974.

A discussion of alcoholism in the homosexual community. The material reported is based on the work of Hank Therholz, founder of "Live and Let Live."

624 "There is a Jewel in this Process, Issues for Lesbian Couples in Recovery: An Interview with Marty Johnson and Mary Brandish." Out From Under. Ed. Jean Swallow. San Francisco: Spinsters, Ink, 1983. 102-16.

A very good discussion of various issues couples need to address when one (or both) enter a recovery program. Johnson and Brandish are both therapists who work with lesbian couples who share their own expriences as a couple where one is an alcoholic and the other a co-alcoholic.

625 Therholz, Hank. "The Alcoholic Gay--Stigma and Sobriety." National Alcoholism Forum, Denver, 29 April 1974.

Given the same month that the American Psychiatric Association removed homosexuality from its list of illnesses, this paper gives much general information on homosexuality.

626 Thomas, John. "A Gay Member's Eye View of Alcoholics Anonymous." National Council on Alcoholism Annual Meeting, Seattle, May 1980.

Thomas adopts the concepts in A Member's Eye View of Alcoholic's Anonymous to a gay and lesbian audience. He also discusses how AA not only helped him sober up but also helped him become comfortable with his homosexuality. He also offers the comment that "Equally significant is the influence of AA on the gay world around it....Gay AA is providing one of the few role models available to the gay world that says: you can be gay without obsessive social drinking..."

627 Thomas, S. "Seriousness and Sobriety." Lesbian Contradiction 10 (1985): 5.

This article is cited in The Alternative Press Index 17.2 (1985): 3.

628 Thomas, Sherry. "The Sober Dyke." Out From Under. Ed. Jean Swallow. San Francisco: Spinsters, Ink, 1983: 221-34.

Thomas discusses how, while loving a "sober dyke," she was able to first confront her own feelings as an adult child of an alcoholic and then face her own alcohol problem.

629 Thomas, Timothy P. "The Fear of Being Positive." NALGAP News 7.4 (1986): 8.

Using his personal experience, Thomas discusses the fear one experiences while waiting for the results of the HTLV-III test.

630 ---. "Gay Alcoholism Education Program." Cleveland: Regional Council on Alcoholism, [1985].

A statement of how the Cleveland Regional Council on Alcoholism hopes to address the issue of alcoholism in the homosexual community.

631 ---. "The Prevention of Alcohol Abuse in the Gay Community." Cleveland: Regional Council on Alcoholism, [1985].

Proposes a five step program for preventing alcoholism in the homosexual community.

632 Ticktin, Stephen. "David Cooper: A Personal Portrait." Body Politic 6 (1972): 4.

A portrait of Dr. David Cooper, author of Death in the Family. Ticktin focusses on what, to him, is the "paradoxical nature of David's alcoholism."

633 Tilchen, M. "Alcohol Conference Held in Bar Here." Gay Community News 12 April 1980: 3.

An explanation of the services offered by the Women's Alcoholism Program of the Cambridge and Somerville Program for Alcoholism Rehabilitation, Inc.

634 ---. "Lesbian AA Conference to Convene." Gay Community News 11 October 1980: 11.

This article is cited in The Alternative Press Index 12.4 (1980): 2.

635 ---. "Women's Alcohol Program Helps Lesbians." Gay Community News 7 May 1983: 6.

This article is cited in The Alternative Press Index 15.2 (1983): 2.

636 "To Keep From Being Controlled: An Interview with Misha Cohen." Out From Under. Ed. Jean Swallow. San Francisco: Spinsters, Ink, 1983. 71-78.

Cohen is an acupuncturist and naturopathic healer. The interview focuses on Chinese medicine.

637 "To Your Health: Improving Immunity." Gay News-Telegraph 5.5 (1986): 11.

Encouragement is given to avoid drugs and alcohol.

638 "Treatment Recommendation." NAGAP Newsletter 4.1/2 (1982-83): 7.

The article summarizes the points in: Grace, John. Coming Out Alive: A Positive Development Model of Homosexual Competence. Minneapolis: Sober Alternative, 1982.

639 Tsui, Kitty. "In Training." Out From Under. Ed. Jean Swallow. San Francisco: Spinters, Ink, 1983. 34-43.

Story of a woman who used weight training to help her stop using drugs.

640 Tucker, A. "Point is Control." Off Our Backs 3.3 (1972): 29.

The article is cited under the alcoholism category in The Alternative Press Index 4.4 (1972): 2.

641 Turner, William J. Letter. "Alcoholism, Homosexuality, and Bipolar Affective Disorder." American Journal of Psychiatry 138 (1981): 262-63.

The letter presents the case history of a woman who had a homosexual brother and an alcoholic father.

642 12 Ways Pride Institute Helps You Better Serve Your Alcoholic and Drug Dependent Gay and Lesbian Patients. Eden Prairie, MN: Pride Institute, [1986].

Title is self-explanatory. Pride Institute is located at 14400 Martin Drive, Eden Prairie, MN 55344.

643 "Two AA Groups Serve the Gay Community." The Illuminator 10 (1985): [2].

This article announces the formation of the Lambda Group and the Sobriety Society in Fort Wayne. The Lambda Group serves homosexuals interested in AA and Al-Anon while the Sobriety Society is strictly AA. The article discusses some of the principles of AA as well as the high rate of alcoholism in the homosexual community.

644 "Two New Articles by NAGAP Author." NAGAP Newsletter 4.1/2 (1982-83): 6-7.

The article is a one passage each from Peter M. Nardi's "Alcoholism and Homosexuality: A Theoretical Perspective" and "Alcohol and the Non-Traditional 'Family' Structures of Gays and Lesbians."

645 Ugolnik, Elaine. "Lancaster's Gays: A Community With Low Profile." Lancaster Sunday News 13 May 1984: 1A+.

Alcohol use is mentioned in this article.

646 Underhill, Brenda L. "Elements of Effective Services for the Lesbian Alcoholic." Sobering Thoughts 2.1 (1982): 5-10.

Underhill's thesis is that "the barriers to effective treatment for the lesbian who seeks help are largely cultural and external, not intra-psychic and internal. After listing six problems for which treatment professionals must be aware, she discusses how these problems might be addressed. Underhill concludes that "all of us in human services need to act as advocates for our lesbian clients."

647 ---. "Lesbianism and Alcoholism: A Selected Bibliography." Los Angeles: Alcoholism Center for Women, nd.

Includes listings on lesbianism, alcoholism, and lesbian alcoholics.

648 Unitarian Universalist Lesbian/Gay Word April/May 1983.

A special issue on women and alcoholism. See "Alcoholism and You," "Alcoholism Defined," "Case Histories in Drinking," David's "Case History," DJ's "What the Family Can Do to Help," "Drinking Myths," Cindy Campman's "'Ramblings' With the Editor," and "Women and Alcoholism."

649 V., Larry. "Glamour Queen from the Midwest..." RFD 28 (1981): 38.

Larry tells what his life had been like, what happened, and what life for him is like today. He concludes his story: "My addiction has been a bridge into a fellowship in AA and to all my abilities in myself. My life sober is the most precious thing that I have."

650 V., Rachel. A Women Like You: Life Stories of Women Recovering from Alcoholism and Addiction. San Francisco: Harper and Row, 1985.

The book includes Malinda P.'s "Malinda P."

651 Vachon, Ron. "Dual Diagnosis: AIDS and Chemical Dependency." The Committee on a National Strategy for AIDS, New York City, 15 May 1986.

Vachon emphasizes the co-factor of alcoholism to AIDS and the high rate of alcoholism in the lesbian/gay community.

652 Vachon, Ron and Gary Lewis, eds. Facilities and Services Directory. New York: New York Department of Public Health, 1986.

A directory of facilities which provide services to lesbian and gay clients. This publication was commissioned by the National Association of Lesbian and Gay Alcoholism Professionals.

653 VanDerzee, Dawn and Allen L. Ralston. "Gay and Lesbian Substance Abuse: Issues and Answers." Oversight Committee of the Ohio Recovery Council, 1 June 1984.

The thesis of this report is that "gay and lesbian substance abusers represent a large percentage of all substance abusers; yet the chronic problem of abuse in this community has historically all but been ignored." Recommendations are offered as to how the needs of homosexuals might be met.

654 Virga, Vincent. A Comfortable Corner. New York: Avon, 1982.

The major theme in this novel is co-addiction in the gay community.

655 Volpe, Joan. "Links to Sobriety." Alcohol Health and Research World (Winter 1979/80): 39-44.

In her study of a women's halfway house, Volpe writes that "Lesbianism and promiscuity are frowned upon."

656 Voltz, Karen. "Womanrest: Sometimes in Sobriety You Have to Make Big Changes." Out from Under. Ed. Jean Swallow. San Francisco: Spinsters, Ink, 1983: 170-76.

Volz discusses her life of recovery and the need for Womanrest, a chem-free "resort" she founded in Wisconsin.

657 Vourakis, C. "Homosexuals in Substance Abuse Treatment." Substance Abuse: Pharmacologic, Developmental, and Clinical Perspectives. Ed. G. Bennett, C. Vourakis, and D.S. Woolf. New York: John Wiley and Sons, 1983.

This chapter will examine alcohol and other drug abuse among homosexuals within the context of society's attitutdes toward gay people in general. Under the same rubric, the treatment needs of this population will be explored."

658 Vous croyez-vous different? trans. Service de la Littérature AA du Québec. Montreal: Service de la Littérature du Québec, 1979.

Translation of Do You Think You're Different?

659 W[are], Cade. "Bridging the Communications Gap with Gay Alcoholics." North American Congress on Alcohol and Drug Problems, San Francisco, 17 December 1974.

Written from the point of view of a recovering gay alcoholic.

660 W., Ted. "Alcoholism: A Gay Drunks Sobering Story" Advocate 5 March 1981: 18-19.

Ted's article focuses on alcoholism in the gay community and recovery through AA. Special focus is given to gay groups within AA where "many of us learn for the first time that it was our drunkenness and not our homosexuality that turned people off." (quoted from AA's The Homosexual Alcoholic The special treatment needs of homosexual alcoholics are listed and the article ends with a list of recommended readings.

661 Wall, J.A. "A Study of Alcoholism in Women." American Journal of Psychiatry 93 (1937): 943:52.

Ten percent of Wall's subjects reported that they had had at least some overt homosexual experience.

662 Waterson, A.P. "Acquired Immune Deficiency Syndrome." British Medical Journal 5 March 1983: 743-46.

Waterson, in part, evaluates the theory that drug abuse

is "the common denominator between non-homosexuals and the main mass of AIDS patients."

663 The Way Back: The Stories of Gay and Lesbian Alcoholics. 1981. Washington, DC: Whitman-Walker Clinic, 1982.

The stories of five gay men and five lesbians who sobered up though AA. [see "No Place to Hide," "Silver and Sobriety," "A Seminarian's Story," "Streets, Jail, the Mental Ward," "Sailor's Return," "A Better Kind of Music," "He Sets His Own Stage," "Liberated Woman," "Something Was Missing," and "Mother on the Run."]

664 Weathers, Brenda. "Alcoholism and the Lesbian Community." Alcoholism in Women. Ed. C.C. Eddy and J.L. Ford. Dubuque, IA: Kendall/Hunt, 1980. 142-49.

Weathers identifies three major factors at the core of the problem of lesbian alcoholics. "1) the community is an oppressed minority; 2) the lesbian bar is the traditional setting for social activities; and 3) alcoholism service agencies lack responsiveness to the lesbian alcoholic." Each problem is discussed in detail.

665 Weijl, Simon. "Theoretical and Practical Aspects of Psychoanalytic Therapy of Problem Drinkers." Quarterly Journal of Studies on Alcohol 5 (1944): 200-11.

Weijl takes a Freudian view of alcoholism. He places emphasis on the latent homosexual drives that can cause alcoholism. The article does provide a good overview of research in the field.

666 Weil, Maury. "Help Wanted, Advocates Needed." NAGAP Newsletter 5.3 (1984): 3.

In asking for people to write letters of support, Weil explains the suggestions NAGAP made to the National Institute on Alcohol Abuse and Alcoholism.

667 Weinberg, M.S. and C.J. Willams. Male Homosexuals: Their Problems and Adaptation. New York: Oxford University Press, 1974.

The authors give some general descriptions about gay bars in New York, San Francisco, Amsterdam, and Denmark.

668 Weinberg, Thomas S. "Alcohol Use Among Gay Men." Annual Meeting of the Society for the Study of Social Problems, Detroit, 27-30 August 1983.

"The drinking behavior of a sample of forty-six male homosexuals in a southern California city is presented....Respondents varied from those who drank little to self-avowed alcoholics."

669 Wellisch, David K., G.G. DeAngelis, and Carl Paternite. "A Study of Therapy of Homosexual Adolescent Drug Users in a Residential Treatment Setting." Adolescence 16 (1981): 689-700.

A study of 14 homosexual adolescents who received treatment at Pride House, a residential treatment facility in Van Nuys, California.

670 West, Karen. "Really Down: Beyond the Kick." Advocate 30 June 1976: 21-23.

West describes "poly-drug abuse," the process of mixing a variety of mood altering chemicals with or without alcohol. Her thesis is that "we must stop numbing symptoms and deal with the causes of our pains." Good use of interviews.

671 Wheelan, Mary. "The Line." Out from Under. Ed. Jean Swallow. San Francisco: Spinsters, Ink, 1983. 25-6.

This poem demonstrates the struggle of "walking both sides of the line" of sobriety.

672 White, L. "It Isn't Easy Being Gay." *Women in Treatment: Issues and Approaches*. Ed. A. Bauman. Arlington: National Drug Abuse Center, 1976.

White investigates issues lesbians face in substance abuse treatment programs.

673 Whitlock, Barbara. Rev. of *Out From Under*, by Jean Swallow. *Off Our Backs* 14.5 (1984): 21.

In her review, Whitlock writes: "The book is an anthology of personal narratives, dramatizations, interviews, poems, novel excerpts, and journal entries....The book also contains the experiences of lesbians who are friends, lovers, and children of lesbians." Whitlock is favorably impressed with the book.

674 Whitney, Scott. "The Ties that Bind: Strategies for Counseling the Gay Male Co-Alcoholic." *Journal of Homosexuality* 7.4 (1982): 37-42.

"This article is an attempt to describe a theoretical model for viewing co-addiction with a more specific discussion of how this model applies to gay male relationships."

675 Wholey, C.C. "Revelations of the Unconscious in a Toxic (Alcoholic) Psychosis." *American Journal of Insanity* 74 (1918): 437-447.

In his case study, Wholey writes that "The patient's overwhelming money complex revealing itself so dramatically in his psychosis, together with the marked obstinacy, orderliness, and punctiliousness characterizing the individual, present evidence of the relationship of chronic alcoholism with homosexuality and anal eroticism."

676 Wholey, Dennis. *The Courage to Change: Hope and Help for Alcoholics and Their Families*. Boston: Houghton Mifflin, 1984.

Wholey's chapter on "Homosexuality and Alcoholism" includes the story of Robert Bauman's recovery and ignores lesbianism. Reference to homosexuality is also found in Graham Chapman's story. [see Robert Bauman and Graham Chapman]

677 Willenbecher, Thom. "The Bush League: The Rites and Rituals of Shadow Sex." Advocate 6 March 1980: 16-18.

While discussing compulsive sexual activity, Willenbecher writes: "Some therapists compare this [compulsive] pursuit [of sex] to alcoholism and other addictions."

678 Williams, Bob. "Downers, Uppers, and Hallucinogens." Advocate 30 June 1976: 24-5.

A general discussion "of some of the drugs commonly used in the gay community" with special emphasis on pharmaceuticals.

679 Williams, K.H. "Overview of Sexual Problems in Alcoholism"." Workshop on Sexual Counseling for Persons with Alcohol Problems. Pittsburgh, 1976.

Williams briefly mentions homosexuality.

680 Williams, Kathy. "Bars Only Place Homosexuals Can Go to Be Themselves." The Evening Times 20 January 1981: B1+.

In her discussion of gay bars, Williams comments on the fact that alcoholism is prevalent in the homosexual community. AA is also mentioned.

681 Willowroot, Abby. "Creativity, Politics, and Sobriety." Out From Under. Ed. Jean Swallow. San Francisco: Spinsters, Ink, 1983: 122-28.

Willowroot writes that: "Cultural conditioning keeps wimmin from valuing themselves and each other. Much of the message is designed to keep wimmin consuming in order to feel better about themselves and boost the economy. Happy people are lousy consumers. When wimmin feel good about themselves, they are not looking for external fixes."

682 Wilsnack, Sharon C. and L. Beckman, eds. Alcohol Problems in Women. New York: Guilford Press, 1984.

Includes S.C. Wilsnack's "Drinking, Sexuality, and Sexual Dysfunction in Women."

683 Wilsnack, Sharon C. "Drinking, Sexuality, and Sexual Dysfunction in Women." Alcohol Problems in Women. Ed. Sharon C. Wilsnack and L. Beckwith. New York: Guilford Press, 1984. 75-89.

A section on "Drinking and Sexual Orientation" gives an overview on research in the field.

684 ---. "Prevention of Alcohol Problems in Women" unpublished manuscript.

"Sexual Orientation" is mentioned as one area in which alcoholic women can have problems.

685 Wilson, G. Terrence and David M. Lawson. "Expectancies, Alcohol, and Sexual Arousal in Women." Journal of Abnormal Psychology 87 (1978): 358-67.

In their study of the relationship of alcohol on measured sexual arousal, both heteroerotic and homoerotic films were used.

686 "Women and Alcoholism." Unitarian Universalist Lesbian/Gay Word April/May 1983: 1-2.

A general overview of alcoholism and how it affects women. Lesbianism is not specifically discussed.

687 "Women and Drug/Alcohol Abuse." Feminist Bookstore News 7.1 (1983): 25-26.

A booklist that includes titles of particular interest to lesbians. The introductory pargraphs include a reference to lesbian alcoholics.

688 "Women's Project Serves Lesbian Clients." Alcoholism Education and Training News 2.6 (1979): 5.

Reprinted from the National Institute on Alcohol Abuse and Alcoholism IFS (#23, April 12, 1976) this article describes Los Angeles' Alcoholism Program for Women.

689 Woods, Colmcille P. "Alcohol Abuse Among Lesbians: An Investigation of Possible Contributing Factors." Dissertation. U.S. International University, 1981.

The study identified factors that were associated with alcohol abuse in the lesbian population.

690 Wynne, Jeffrey, D. "A Brief Overview of Gay Problem Drinking in San Diego, California in the 1980's." unpublished paper.

"The primary purpose of this paper is to provide a brief overview of gay problem drinking in San Diego County. The paper is further designed to provide insight into the magnitude of gay problem drinking and, in that process, should help to demystify some of the misconceptions and lies about homosexuality and homosexual behavior."

691 Yarrow. "Chem Free Space." Off Our Backs 14.5 (1984): 21.

Yarrow believes that "The most frequent reaction to the idea of chem-free space in the Lesbian community has been one of either defensiveness or anger; defensiveness of the kind when I feel that someone else is doing something that I feel I should be doing but am not....The anger is usually of the sort, 'No one is going to tell me what I can or can't do.'" She then discusses the positive aspects of providing a chem free space.

692 Young, Dick. "Alcoholism Higher Among Gays, But Treatment Lags." The Seattle Times 4 May 1980: C5.

A brief summary of Lilene Fifield's "Key Note Speech."

693 Zehner, Martha Ann and Joyce Lewis. "Homosexuality and Alcoholism: Social and Developmental Perspectives." Homosexuality and Social Work. Ed. R. Schoenberg, S. Goldberg, and D.A. Shore. New York: Haworth Press, 1984. 75-89.

"The article is divided into three areas: a general description and definition of alcoholism as a problem in our society; special issues for gays and lesbians and their vulnerability to alcoholism; services for alcoholics generally and services geared specifically to lesbian and gay alcoholics."

694 Ziebold, Thomas O. "Alcoholism and Recovery: Gays Helping Gays." Christopher Street 3.6 (1979): 36-44.

An in depth discussion of the stigma of being homosexual and alcoholic, the disease aspect of alcoholism, and the availability and lack of availability of alcohol treatment facilities. He concludes that "If the gay community would adopt a stance of 'taking care of its own' in developing effective alcoholism prevention and treatment programs, it would demonstrate a high degree of gay pride at work." (44) References and suggested readings follow the article.

695 ---. "Alcoholism and Recovery: Gays Helping Gays*." PLGTF Bulletin 3.9 (1981): 6-7+.

An excerpt from his Christopher Street article of the same title.

696 ---. "Alcoholism and the Gay Community." The Blade March 1978: n.p.

A good, general discussion of the disease of alcoholism and how it affects the homosexual community.

697 ---. "Alcoholism is an Illness; Not a Sin." RFD 28 (1981): 26-27.

Reprint of "Alcoholism and Recovery: Gays Helping Gays."

698 ---. "Ethical Issues in Substance Abuse Treatment Relevant to Sexual Minorities." Eagleville Conference, Pennsylvania, 11 May 1979.

Ziebold concludes that comfortable sobriety "can only be achieved in an atmosphere of acceptance and assistance of the gay man or lesbian in exploring what it means to be gay....For the chemically dependent person, the beginning of their existence as a male, gay person usually begins with sobriety. The process requires careful nurture as part of recovery treatment."

699 ---. "Ethical Issues in Substance Abuse Treatment Relevant to Sexual Minorities." Contemporary Drug Problems 8 (1979): 413-18.

Published version of conference paper of same title.

700 ---. Ways to Gay Sobriety: Recovery Strategies for Homosexual Alcoholics in Recovery and Reconstruction. Washington, D.C.: Gay Council on Drinking Behavior, Whitman-Walker Clinic, 1981.

Ziebold proposes strategies for treating alcoholism in the homosexual community.

701 Ziebold, Thomas O. and John E. Mongeon. Alcoholism and Homosexuality. New York: Haworth Press, 1982.

A special issue of the Journal of Homosexuality which has been republished under the title Gay and Sober.

[see William E. Bittle, Ronnie W. Colcher, Rosanne Driscoll, Emily B. McNally, John Mongeon, Peter Nardi, Tom Mills Smith, Scott Whitney, and Tricia A. Zigrang]

702 ---. "Introduction: Alcoholism in the Homosexual Community." Journal of Homosexuality 7.4 (1982): 1-9.

The article serves as an introduction to Ziebold and Mongeon's Alcoholism and Homosexuality by giving a brief overview of the problem.

703 Zigrang, Tricia A. "Who Should Be Doing What About the Gay Alcoholic?" Journal of Homosexuality 7.4 (1982): 27-36.

"Treatment options for the homosexual alcoholic are examined with the conclusion that increased education for staff about the particular needs of homosexual alcoholics and development of specialized services in existing treatment facilities are high priorities." An in-service training format and directions for further research are also presented.

704 Zon, Kate. "Roseburg Has a Gay AA Group." RFD 35 (1983): 47.

A general discussion of how one gay AA group formed and continues to operate.

705 Zwerling, I. and M. Rosenbaum. "Alcohol Addiction and Personality." American Handbook of Psychiatry. Ed. S. Arieti. New York: Basic Books, 1959: 623-44.

Zwerling cites homosexuality as a cause of alcoholism.

SELECTED BIBLIOGRAPHY ON

LESBIAN AND GAY ISSUES

In this section of the NALGAP Annotated Bibliography we have compiled a list of resource materials on lesbian and gay issues because we are aware that many treatment professionals who to learn more about gay/lesbian issues are unaware of what is available. Also, it is often necessary to direct individuals in the early stages of the coming out process to materials which will assist them. Following are some of the best and most available sources for information on homosexuality.

General Sources on Lesbian/Gay Issues

706 Abbott, Sidney and Barbara Love. Sappho Was a Right-On Woman: A Liberated View of Lesbianism. 1972; New York: Stein and Day, 1983.

Abbott and Love separate the book into two sections. They write in the introduction, "In the first half we mean to say, perhaps especially to our younger sisters, in whom we see a new pride emerging, remember never to forget that Gay Liberation is the result of an historical process. In the second half we want to reflect the full pride Lesbians are striving for, although few have yet achieved it." Although the book was written over a decade ago, it remains an important statement on the relationship between lesbianism and feminism.

707 Adair, Nancy and Casey Adair. Word is Out: Stories of Some of Our Lives. New York: Dell Publishing and San Francisco: New Glide Publications, 1978.

The material for this book was put together from material collected for the film Word is Out which presented the stories of twenty-six lesbian women and gay men. Twenty-four of those people are interviewed for this book which also includes a narrative of Nancy Adair's story. One of the noteworthy strengths of this book is balance. Men and women from various races, socio-economic backgrounds, ages, and political backgrounds are included. Also, the reader is permitted to listen to each individual's words while they respond to the interviewer's questions. There are no summaries or editorial commentaries to interfere with the book's basic message: there is a diversity in our experience. A selected bibliography complete with brief annotations concludes the book.

708 Archtenberg, Roberta, ed. Sexual Orientation and the Law New York: Clark Boardman Company, Ltd., 1985.

Sexual Orientation and the Law is the most definitive work available on lesbain/gay legal issues.

709 Berzon, Betty and Robert Leighton, eds. Positively Gay. Millbrae, CA: Celestial Arts, 1979.

The book promises to give new approaches to "family relationships, mental health, religion, coupling, aging, job security, financial planning, political organizing, and more." And it delivers what it promises. Chapters range from Betty Berzon's "Developing a Positive Gay Identity" to Douglas C. Knutson's "Job Security for Gays: Legal Aspects." Other issues specifically addressed are financial planning, parents of gays, voting power, and coming out. Berzon and Leighton have achieved a balance in Positively Gay that is seldom found in lesbian/gay publications. There are separate chapters on being a lesbian mother and a gay father as well as on the older lesbian and the older gay men. And instead of finding someone to write a single chapter on religion and homosexuality, they have included Brian McNaught's "Gay and Catholic," Barrett L. Brick's "Judaism in the Gay Community," and Bill Johnson's "Protestantism and Gay Freedom."

710 Brown, Howard. Familiar Faces Hidden Lives: The Story of Homosexual Men in America Today. New York: Harcourt, Brace, Jovanovich, 1976.

In this autobiography, Brown, the first chief health officer of New York City, tells how he came to accept his homosexuality. Because Brown was a physician, his story would particularly appeal to homosexual professionals.

711 Califia, Pat. Sapphistry: The Book of Lesbian Sexuality. 1980; Tallahassee, FL: Niad, 1983.

In her forward to Sapphistry, Phyllis Lyon writes that the book "not only discusses the broad range of sexual behavior possible between women, but it does so in a non-judgmental and realistic way. Pat Califia understands the need for communication, for caring and for sharing between women. She also understands the diversity of Lesbians, and that what you choose to do sexually is okay. There are no performance standards." Califia writes that: "Our sexuality can be a source of pleasure, nourishment and strength." The book is designed to aid in the nourishment. Chapters include material on the erotic imagination, self-loving, partners, communication, common sexual concerns, youth, age, and sex, disabled lesbians, sexually transmitted diseases, and passion. A resource list is also available.

712 Clark, Don. Living Gay. Millbrae, CA: Celestial Arts, 1979.

Living Gay is Clark's sequel to Loving Someone Gay and unlike most sequels it not only has the same vitality as the first book but it also contributes further to a person's growth and development. In describing the book, Clark explains that it is "about living, loving, loving aging and dying as seen from a gay perspective." And this perspective is specifically viewed through Clark's own experience and the experience of his friends and clients. Chapters range from discussions of parenting (both for lesbians and gay men as well as heterosexuals with homosexual children), humor, sex, and the ceremony and celebration of lesbian/gay life. The chapter which explains why "Every Man Should Own a Dress" is a perfect example of how Clark can give a serious presentation on such experiences as sexism or internalized homophobia without taking himself or his subject matter too seriously.

713 ---. Loving Someone Gay. 1977. New York: Signet Classics, 1978.

In the introduction to Loving Someone Gay, Clark writes that: "If you care about someone who is Gay, are Gay yourself, or think you might be, this book is for you. The first chapter explains the setting--how it is to be Gay today in our part of the world. The second chapter offers suggestions for making it a more growth filled experience. The third chapter talks to fathers, mothers, husbands, wives, brothers, sisters, good friends, and others who love someone Gay and want to know how to become better related. The final chapter is for professionals who want to improve their work with Gay people." Much of the strength of the book is found in the fact that Clark is willing to share his experiences as a gay man and a gay professional as well as the experiences of his friends and clients. The reader learns more about himself as he comes to know Don and the people in Don's life. For many, this contact with Don is their first exposure to a healthy, happy, gay man.

714 Denneny, Michael; Charles Ortleb and Thomas Steele, eds. The Christopher Street Reader. New York: Perigee Books, 1983.

In his introduction, Denneny writes that: "Like a town meeting, a magazine enables people to be in each other's company by sharing talk about matters that concern them. And it is through talking with others that most of us start to make some sense of the world, and begin to discover who we are and what we think." This reader is an attempt to synthesize some of the discussion which had taken place in Christopher Street during its first five years of publication. To accomplish this goal, forty-eight essays have been grouped under five headings: "Living the Life," "State of the Tribe," "Word from Abroad," "Recovering the Past," and "Cultural Politics." The author's include some of the most published writers in the gay male press: Edmund White, Tim Dlugos, Dennis Altman, Randy Shilts, and Andrew Holleran. Subjects range from Aaron Fricke's "One Life, One Prom" to George Stambolian's "Interview with a Fetishist" and from Charles Ortleb's "The Context of Cruising" to Randy Shilt's "The Life and Death of Harvey Milk." Notably absent from the list of authors are any women or specifically women identified issues even though many women have published first-rate articles in the magazine. However, as Denneny explains: "Christopher Street simply has to accept the fact that at the moment it is a gay male magazine."

715 Fricke, Aaron. Reflections of a Rock Lobster: A Story About Growing Up Gay. Boston: Alyson, 1983.

A rock lobster is defined as "1. a crustacean having a firm shell for defense against predators, but lacking claws. 2. a song popular with young people in the early nineteen-eighties." Aaron Fricke was a rock lobster whose request to take a male date to his high school prom became the focus of national attention. Reflection of a Rock Lobster is Fricke's autobiography. Written by a teenager facing typical teeneage events in an atypical fashion, the book has a special appeal to high school students who may themselves be confonting their sexuality.

716 Heger, Heinz. The Men With the Pink Triangle. Trans. David Fernbach. Boston: Alyson, 1980.

Heger writes in his introduction: "The fate of gay people under Nazi rule has been the object of deliberate suppression. Neither in Germany itself, nor in the countries whose armies liberated Europe from the Nazis, did the powers-that-be want it known that homosexuals, too, were the victims of Nazi mass murder. Gay people, though a very distinct category in the concentration camps, were even omitted from memorials erected to the victims of Nazism. Scarcely surprising, since in 1945 male homosexuality was equally illegal in the United States, Britain, and Soviet Russia..." In The Men With the Pink Triangles, Heinz records the history of the "gay genocide."

717 Heron, Ann, ed. One Teenager in 10: Testimony by Gay and Lesbian Youth. 1983. New York: Warner, 1986.

The book is a series of personal testimonials of twenty-seven lesbian/gay young people. The stories which are recorded tell about coming to terms with their sexuality and their courage in facing the truth about themselves and declaring that truth to family, friends, and society. The book is particulary important because it is not adults talking to teenagers, but teenagers talking to each other. The 1986 edition includes an introduction/"pep talk" by Rita Mae Brown. In it, she discusses sexual orienation in the perspective of teenages having to come to terms with sexuality. She also cautions the homosexual teenager not to warp themselves by focusing only on their sexuality. She concludes her introduction with the comment that: "If someone wants to call you a queer, let them. The only people who are queer are the people who don't love anybody. If you remember that, you'll not only survive. You'll triumph."

718 Katz, Jonathan. Gay American History: Lesbians and Gay Men in the U.S.A.. New York: Thomas Y. Crowell, 1977.

Gay American History is an attempt to document "the experience of ordinary Gay people. No particular effort was made to document the lives of homosexuals creative or famous." For the most part the documents re-printed in this collection are allowed to speak for themselves. However, each is prefaced by a brief description. The six sections of the book are "Trouble" (1566-1966), "Treatment" (1884-1974), "Passing Women" (1782-1920), "Native Americans/Gay Americans" (1528-1976), "Resistance" (1859-1972), and "Love" (1779- 1932). There is no overriding theme for the selections either within the collection or within each section. But, the majority of the entries focus on the difficulty of being homosexual in America and the negative results of homophobia.

719 Kopay, David and Perry Deane Young. The David Kopay Story: An Extraordinary Self-Revelation. New York: Arbor House, 1977.

In the foreword, Young writes that the decision to write this book "has not been to serve up a political tract for the cause, but we do hope that it will help in creating more understanding of homosexuals and homosexuality." To do this, they record the story of David Kopay--all American football hero who was co-captain of the University of Washington's 1964 Rose Bowl team and a running back for the San Francisco Forty-Niners, the Detroit Lions, the Washington Redskins, the New Orleans Saints, and the Green Bay Packers--who accepted his homosexuality and confronted church, family, and society as a healthy gay man. The book is particularly interesting because for many individuals, "jocks" such as Kopay seem to be everything that a gay man isn't.

720 Lauritsen, John and David Thorstad. The Early Homosexual Rights Movement (1864-1935). New York: Times Change Press, 1974.

Lauritsen and Thorstad write that: "The aim of this book will be to sketch briefly the history of this early struggle for homosexual rights, its rise and decline, and to discuss some of the issues it raised, with the hope that this will contribute to the gay liberation sturggle today and to the revolutionary movement as a whole." Besides describing the early homosexual rights movement, the authors include chapters on scientific and theoretical issues, socialism and the early gay movement, regeneration, and additional notes on five pioneers: Karl Heinrich Ulrichs, Magnus Hirschfeld, Sir Richard Burton, Walt Whitman, and Edward Carpenter.

721 Loulan, JoAnn. Lesbian Sex. San Francisco: Spinsters, Ink, 1984.

At the heart of the book is a desire for lesbians to learn about their bodies and how not to permit barriers from interfering with sexuality and sexual enjoyment. Loulan begins by explaining issues of sexuality and homophobia as well as presenting factual information about the body's physiology. In chapters such as "The Tyranny of Orgasm" and "Sexual Addiction" issues which inhibit sexual fulfillment are presented. Recognizing that life is a process of change and growth, information is presented on coming out, being single, and relationships. Sections of the text also explain the relationship between sex and disability, motherhood, sobriety, aging, and youth. Of special significance is the fact that Loulan includes a chapter that gives exercises which a woman or a couple can do to improve communication, increase relaxation, decrease homophobia, improve self-love and love of partner, and enhance desire. Exercises are also included for learning the dynamics of sexual desire while becoming comfortable with your own and your partners genitals. Specific sexual exercises are also given as are exercises directed at survivors and partners of such sexual abuse as incest or rape. These exercises are cited throughout the text. Lesbian Sex includes drawings by Barbara Johnson and technical drawings by Marcia Quackenbush. Marny Hall has supplied a section on "Lesbians, Limerance, and Longterm Relationships" and Jill Lessing has contributed a section on "Sex and Disability."

722 Martin, Del and Phyllis Lyon. Lesbian/Woman. 1972. New York: Bantam, 1983.

Often touted as a modern classic, the purpose of Lesbian/Woman is to record "the everyday life experience of the Lesbian: how she views herself as a person; how she deals with the problems she encounters in her various roles as a woman, worker, friend, parent, child, citizen, wife, employer, welfare recipient, home owner and taxpayer; and how she views other people and the world around her." Martin and Lyon have lived together as lovers for nineteen years before writing this book. They have been active in the Daughters of Bilitis since it was founded in 1955 and have been deeply involved in other aspects of the homophile movement. They emphasize the difference between homosexual and homophile by explaining that homosexual uses the Greek derivation of homo which means "sex with the same" whereas homophile uses the Latin derivation to mean "love of same." By placing "sex" in the proper perspective in homosexual, the authors record the experience of lesbians in such a way that those who do not yet identify with the lesbian community can come to terms with the positive aspect of their sexuality. Lesbian/Woman was revised and expanded for the 1983 edition which is available in paperback.

723 McWhirter, David P. and Andrew M. Mattison. The Male Couple: How Relationships Develop. Englewood Cliffs: Prentice-Hall, 1984.

McWhirter and Mattison's study is based on interviews with 156 gay male couples over the course of five years. These couples had been together from one to thirty-seven years. As a result of their research, the authors discovered that gay couples tend to grow through six predictable stages: 1) blending, 2) nesting, 3) maintaining, 4) building, 5) releasing, and 6) renewing. They explain each of these stages and cite many examples from the lives of the men they interviewed. The book concludes with a detailed description of the study, the individuals who participated in it, and general comments on everyday life, family, friends, social life, and sexuality. Recommendations are also given for further research. The authors are careful to explain that "the very nature of our research sample, it size (156 couples), its narrow geographic location, and the natural selectiveness of the participants prevent the findings from being applicable and generalizable to the entire gay male community." However, they do dispel many myths about gay couples and lay the groundwork for further, more comprehensive studies.

724 Muchmore, Wes and William Hanson. Coming Out Right: A Handbook for the Gay Male. Boston: Alyson Publications, 1982.

In Coming Out Right, Muchmore and Hanson give an overview of the gay male community. Because they recognize that gay experience is varied, they attempt to present non-biased explanations of what people actually do. For example, the authors present material on gay bars, baths, cruising places, male prostitutes, and new alternatives. And although they discuss the dangers of possible activities, they refrain from making ethical judgements. The book is a survey of gay experience for the man who is just accepting his sexual orientation and is attempting to break into the gay lifestyle. It shows him what others have done but encourages him to make his own decisions. The authors acknowledge that: "Much of the information we present is neither cheering nor pretty. In such concentrated form it may tend to give a negative, even frightening view of gay existence. This is an unavoidable distortion." But, a man who reads this book and is able to discuss it with someone with more experience in the gay community will gain valuable insight into himself and the world into which he is entering.

725 O'Donnell, Mary, Kater Pollock, Val Leoffler, and Ziesel Saunders. Lesbian Health Matters!: A Resource Book About Lesbian Health. Santa Cruz: Santa Cruz Women's Health Center, 1979.

Lesbian Health Matters is written as a reaction to the heterosexism of the health care system. Chapters include information on gynecological health, alternative fertilization, menopause, alcoholism and co-alcoholism, taking care of ourselves, feminist therapy, and towards better lesbian health care. The Santa Cruz Women's Health Center is located at 250 Locust Street, Santa Cruz, CA 95060.

726 Silverstein, Charles and Edmund White. The Joy of Gay Sex: An Intimate Guide for Gay Men to the Pleasures of a Gay Lifestyle. New York: Simon and Schuster, 1977.

The Joy of Gay Sex is included in this bibliography not so much as a recommendation but as an acknowledgement that it is popular. Unfortunately, the text has not been updated since it was published in 1977. Safe-sex practices are not discussed and, as a result, much of the sexual activity described could be dangerous. Also, the authors take a fairly casual attitude toward substance use/abuse.

727 Sisley, Emily and Bertha Harris. The Joy of Lesbian Sex: A Tender and Liberated Guide to the Pleasures and Problems and Problems of a Lesbian Lifesstyle. New York: Simon and Schuster, 1977.

The Joy of Lesbian Sex is written in a dictionary format where the authors are able to define with examples and commentary various terms relevant to lesbianism, lesbian sexuality, and lesbian sexual activity.

728 Stoddard, Thomas, et al. _The Rights of Gay People_. 1975. New York: Bantam, 1983.

The Rights of Gay People is a series of questions and answers categorized under ten headings: freedom of speech and association: the right to organize and speak out, the right to equal employment opportunities, occupational licenses, the armed services, security clearances, immigration and naturalization, housing and public accommodations, the gay family, gays and the criminal law, and the rights of transvestites and transsexuals. Six appendixes are also included: criminal statutes relating to consensual homosexual acts between adults, a bibliography of works on law and civil rights of interest to gays, antidiscrimination laws of Minneapolis, Minnesota and East Lansing, Michigan, executive orders of the governors of California and Pennsylvania, a selective list of gay organizations, and ACLU state affiliates. (In the book, gay is defined to mean both men and women.) The book is written for non-lawyers and can be used to help people understand that gay men and lesbians do have rights. As the authors write in the introduction to the first edition, an introduction which also appears in the second edition: "If there is a single, overriding lesson that emerges from the discussion that follows, it is that gay people do have a great many rights--indeed, the same rights as all other members of society--but that these rights take on significance only to the extent that they are intelligently and knowledgeably exercised."

729 Swallow, Jean, ed. _Out From Under: Sober Dykes and Our Friends_. San Francisco: Spinsters, Ink, 1983.

Focusing on the recovery process which lesbians have used to keep sober, Swallow divides her book into four sections: the days of our recovery, the healers among us, the politics of addiction, and the way forward. The book has been included in the annotated bibliography on homosexuality and alcoholism with individual entries included for each contributor.

730 Wolfe, Susan J. and Julia Penelope Stanley, ed. The Coming Out Stories. Watertown, MA: Persephone Press, 1980.

In their introduction, Wolfe and Stanley write that: "This book exists because wimmin love wimmin. In spite of persistent denials from our culture that lesbianism is real, each of us has found her way to the love of self and other wimmin. Claiming a Lesbian identity has been easy for some, a long and tortured journey for others; some wimmin have loved a womon and only years later decided that they are Lesbians, while others have discovered their lesbianism and then set out to seek other Lesbians. However, we have arrived at our Lesbian identity, whatever labels we have donned and shed in the process, we have eventually discovered ourselves in a society that denies our existence." The Coming Out Stories is a collection of 41 stories of women who have arrived at a Lesbian identity. As the experiences of self discovery are varied within the Lesbian community, the stories in this collection are no less varied.

Parents of Lesbians/Gays and Lesbian/Gay Parents

731 Back, Gloria Guss. Are You Still My Mother? Are You Still My Family New York: Warner Books, 1985.

Back writes that her book was a result of the struggle she faced after her youngest son told her that he was gay; reactions that included "the blow to my ego, the hurt, the bewilderment, the confusion." She tried "to learn, to understand and to come to grips with what it means to be homosexual, to be a parent of a homosexual, and to be homophobic..." By recording her experience, it is Back's hope that "in the not-too-distant future, the Gay child will not have to ask, 'Are you still my mother?' or 'Are you still my family?' The book not only include's Back's story, but more general reactions from parents, children, and some experts. She also includes an outline for a six week workshop for families of gay/lesbian people so that they can come to a better understanding of the subject.

732 Borhek, Mary V. Coming Out to Parents: A Two-Way Survival Guide for Lesbians and Gay Men and Their Parents. New York: Pilgrim Press, 1983.

Borhek is a mother who struggled with the knowledge that her son was gay; a struggle that she recorded in My Son Eric. However, as a result of her journey, she has been able to help parents adjust to the knowledge that their son/daughter isn't heterosexual. And she has been able to help lesbians and gay men better able to prepare for the act of coming out to parents as well as to better understand their parent's reaction to the news. As she writes in the introduction: "[by reading the book] the adult child can gain some understanding of the parents' perspectives and of her or his own adjustment to live. The parent who reads the book will gain a perspective of his or her own life situation as well as that of the same-sex-oriented daughter or son." Chapters include an investigation of why the child wants to come out to his/her parents, preparing for the announcement, issues of grief and how grief can be worked out together as a family, ways to let go, and the fact that parents, too, go through a coming out process. Religious issues are also discussed.

733 ---. My Son Eric: A Mother Struggles to Accept Her Gay Son and Discovers Herself. New York: Pilgrim Press, 1979.

My Son Eric is an account of the coming out process from the mother's point of view. Religious issues are a particular focus in Borhek's experience.

734 Fairchild, Betty and Nancy Hayward. Now That You Know: What Every Parent Should Know About Homosexuality. San Diego: Harcourt Brace Jovanovich, 1979.

Fairchild and Hayward are the co-founders of Parents of Gays, now known as Parents and Friends of Lesbians and Gays. After presenting the initial reaction which parents feel after learning that a son/daughter is homosexual, the authors include chapters on the children's story, the parent's story, what is gay?, homosexual children making their way in the world, homosexual couples, homosexuality and religion, parents and children together, and the group that they formed. Although the book is specifically written by parents to other parents about their work with parents of lesbian/gay children, the homosexual child can learn much from the text.

735 Gantz, Joe. Whose Child Cries: Children of Gay Parents Talk About Their Lives. Rolling Hills Estates, CA: Jalmar Press, 1983.

Gantz records the experiences of members of five families where one or both of the biological parents is homosexual.

736 Hobson, Laura Z. Consenting Adult Garden City: Doubleday and Company, 1975.

Hobson's novel begins when the protagonist receives a letter from her son informing her that he is gay. The book continues with the reactions of family members as they begin to understand the implications of having a gay son in the family. Although the book is not autobiography, many families have been helped by it.

737 Silverstein, Charles. A Family Matter: A Parent's Guide to Homosexuality. New York: McGraw-Hill, 1977.

Silverstein writes that "This book is for families who want to learn how to deal with a homosexual son or daughter, and to come to terms with their own feelings about homosexuality. As far as I know, this is the first book written by a professional (a practicing psychologist) especially for you the family of a homosexual." Because the premise of the book is that the professional is talking to parents, A Family Matter lacks much of the intimacy found in books such as Back's Are You Still My Mother? Are You Still My Family? and Fairchild and Hayward's Now That You Know.

Homosexuality and Religion

738 Batchelor, Edward, Jr. Homosexuality and Ethics New York: Pilgrim Press, 1980.

In Homosexuality and Ethics, Batchelor has compiled a balanced set of documents which present the dominant views toward homosexuality: homosexual acts are intrinsically evil, homosexual acts are essential imperfect, homosexual acts are to be evaluated in terms of their relational significance, and homosexual acts are natural and good. The book also includes a chapter titled "Toward a New Homosexual Ethic" and one that offers various critiques. Contributors for the volume are Roger Shinn, Tom F. Driver, Gergory Baum, Rosemary Ruether, St. Thomas Aquinas, Karl Barth, Robert Gordis, John G. Milhaven, William Muehl, Ruth Tiffany Barnhouse, Charles E. Curran, Helmut Thielicke, H. Kimball Jones, Hershel Matt, W. Norman Pittenger, Michael F. Valente, Neale Secor, Robert W. Wood, James B. Nelson, Theodore W. Jennings, Lisa Sowle Cahill, and an anonymous article from Sh'ma. The book also includes the "Episcopal Dioceses of Michigan Report" and the "British Friends Task Force Report. Homosexuality and Ethics is an excellent resource guide for someone who is trying to understand various religious attitudes toward homosexual sexual behavior. However, it would not be the best resource to give someone who was still questioning his/her sexuality in terms of a religious tradition.

739 Beck, Elizabeth Torten, (ed). Nice Jewish Girls: A Lesbian Anthology. 1982, Trumansburg, NY: The Crossing Press, 1984.

In her opening essay, "Why is this Book Different for All Other Books?," Beck answers her own question by stating that Nice Jewish Girls was written by people who, according to Jewish law, do not exist. The book, then, is a successful attempt to give voice to Jewish lesbians. The essays which Beck has collected are divided into six categories: "If I Am Not Myself, Who Will I Be?" "Jewish Identity: A Coat of Many Colors," "If I am Only for Myself, What Am I?" "That's Funny, You Don't Look Like a Jewish Lesbian," "Family Secrets," and "Appendix: Cast a Critical Eye." The final section of the book is suggestions for further reading. Material that includes the intersection of Judaisim/Lesbianism, the intersection of Jewish Women/Women of Color, Jewish History, Books, Periodicals, Selected Resources, Small Press/Periodical Addresses, Special Issues of Journals and Newsletters Focused Entirely or in Large Part on Jewish Women and Anti-Semitism, and Tapes.

740 Boswell, John. Christianity, Social Tolerance, and Homosexuality: Gay People in Western Europe from the Beginning of the Christian Era to the Fourteenth Century Chicago: The University of Chicago Press, 1980.

Winner of the 1981 American Book Award for History, Christianity, Social Tolerance, and Homosexuality is an historical text that traces the traces the history of homosexuality from points of departure through the Christian tradition, shifting fortunes, and to the rise of intolerance. Sources for the book, which were consulted in the original and all but a few of which were translated by Boswell, range from the historical, liturary, legal, and ecclesiastical. The material is well researched and heavily footnoted. Often, Boswell provides both the original text and the translation for material. A major difficulty for those approaching the book is explained by Boswell in his introduction: "Because the material considered in this volume comprises both a very broad geographical and temporal expanse and many very detailed and technical issues, it has been somewhat difficult to provide a scholarly apparatus of use to all who might desire it and still make the book accessible to the general reader. Specialists may be surprised at explanations of facts or material which seem perfectly obvious, and nonspecialists may find it difficult to wade through dense, recondite notes." A second problem is the absence of women in the material cited. But, as Boswell acknowledges, during the period about which he is writing, most of the sources were written by men and about men. As often as possible, examples of women are cited, "but no one could offset the overwhelming disproportion of data regarding male and female sexuality without deliberate distortion." Because he was unable to fill in material on lesbianism, Judith Brown's Immodest Acts is an important companion piece to Christianity, Social Tolerance, and Homosexuality.

741 Brown, Judith C. Immodest Acts: The Life of a Lesbian Nun in Renaissance Italy New York: Oxford Press, 1986.

Immodest Acts is the biography of Benedetta Carlini (1590-1661), abbess of the Theatine nuns of Pescia. A mystic accused of lesbianism, Sr. Benedetta's story gives one a rare look into lesbian sexuality during a period where sexual activity was virtually ignored. As Brown explains in her introduction, a study of Benedetta's life permits us to "recreate and hold up to examination the social world in which these attitudes flourished." Brown's book makes an excellent companion to Boswell's Christianity, Social Tolerance, and Homosexuality. Although she does not cover the range of material that Boswell does, Brown does much to fill in the missing chapters in his book.

742 Gramick, Jeannine, ed. Homosexuality and the Catholic Church Chicago: Thomas More Press, 1983.

The essays included in this book are based on presentations given at the First National Symposium on

Homosexuality and the Catholic Church. The essays include Brian McNaught's "Reflections of a Gay Catholic," Ann Borden's "Growing Up Lesbian and Catholic," Jeannine Gramick's "New Sociological Theory on Homosexuality," Barbara Zanotti's "Overcoming the Structured Evil of Male Domination and Heterosexism," Robert Nugent's "Homosexuality, Celibacy, Religious Life and Ordination," Theresa Kane's "Civil Rights in a Church of Compassion," Cornelius Hubbuch's "Gay Men and Women in Vowed Life," Charles Curran's "Moral Theology and Homosexuality," and Kenneth McGuire's "Shifting Attitudes toward Homosexuality."

743 Horner, Tom. Homosexuality and the Judeo-Christian Tradition: An Annotated Bibliography. Metuchen, NJ: Scarecrow Press, 1981.

The book is divided into four sections: books, articles and essays, pamphlets and papers, and bibliographies. There is also an appendix on biblical references to homosexuality and one on periodicals of gay religious organizations.

744 Isherwood, Christopher. My Guru and His Disciple 1980; New York: Penguin Books, 1981.

Isherwood writes the following as a forward to his book: "This is neither a complete biography of Swami Prabhavananda nor a full account of my own life between 1939 and 1976. It is my one-sided, highly subjective story of our guru-disciple relationship. Many people who were closely associated with Prabhavananada or with me, during that period, have little or no part in this particular story and therefore appear in it only briefly or not at all." Much of the value of My Guru and His Disciple comes from the very personal, subjective point of view which Isherwood takes. The reader is able to follow a gay man's struggle with his spirituality and then see how spiritual and secular concerns are integrated into Isherwood's life. The book is also important because it involves a non-

Western (specifically non-Christian) approach to the subject matter.

745 McNeill, John J. The Church and the Homosexual New York: Pocket Books, 1976.

Originally published with the *imprimi potest*, McNeill's book is a study of the homosexual Catholic's relationship to God, church, and society. The first section of the text includes material on moral theology and homosexuality, scripture and homosexuality, tradition and homosexuality, tradition and human nature, and the human sciences and homosexuality. Part two works toward a positive approach of moral theology and part three discusses pastoral ministry to the homosexual community. Of particular interest to homosexual Christians is McNeill's careful analysis of biblical prohibitions concerning homosexuality and homosexual sexual conduct.

746 Nugent, Robert, ed. A Challenge to Love: Gay and Lesbian Catholics in the Church New York: Crossroad, 1983.

In his introduction, Bishop Walter E. Sullivan writes that: "Parents and families, theologians and pastors, women and men religious, vocation and formation personnel, gay and lesbian Catholics will all find in these essays a rich source of stimulating and thought-provoking ideas from writers whose knowledge and experience are invaluable to the People of God." The essays are divided into the following categories: societal perspectives, biblical-theological perspectives, pastoral perspectives, and vocational perspectives.

747 Perry, Troy. The Lord is My Shepherd and He Knows I'm Gay. Los Angeles: Nash Publishing, 1972.

The Lord is My Shepard and He Knows I'm Gay is the autobiography of the Reverend Troy Perry, an evangelical minister who founded the Universal Fellowship of Metropolitan Community Churchs, a religious denomination which focuses its ministry around the gay/lesbian community.

748 Scanzoni, Letha and Virginia Ramey Mollenkott. Is the Homosexual My Neighbor?: Another Christian View 1978; San Francisco: Harper and Row, 1980.

The author's begin their preface commenting that "The Question that makes up the title of this book shouldn't be necessary. After all, Jesus made it clear that every person is our neighbor. And the Bible is likewise clear on what our responsibility is to our neighbor. Love." In developing their thesis, the authors not only include material which asks "Who is my neighbor?" but also chapters on the risks and challenges of moral growth, the homosexual as samaritan, stigma and stereotyping, what the bible says, what scientists say, moving from homophobia to understanding, and the debate in American christendom. They conclude the book by proposing a homosexual Christian ethic.

Technical/Professional Materials

749 Bergstrom, Sage and Lawrence Cruz, eds. Counseling Lesbian and Gay Youth: Their Special Lives/Special Needs. New York: National Network of Run Away and Youth Services, Inc., 1983.

Bergstrom and Lawrence write in the introduction: "The format of an anthology was chosen in order to reflect a variety of individual viewpoints as well as a cross cultural and regional perspective. Opinions expressed are those of the individual authors." Chapters include material on myths and stereotypes, the family and the "coming out" process, administration and delivery of social services, special perspectives, national resources, and recommended readings. Individual essays include Scott Wirth's "Coming Out Close to Home," Adele Starr's "Strengths of Families," Timothy Curran's "Special Senior Ball," Mitzi Simmons' "A Lesbian Connection," Sparky Harlan's "Administration of Lesbian and Gay Youth Services," Paul Gibson's "Developing Services for Lesbian and Gay Youth in a Runaway Shelter," William J. Schipp and Patricia Vivian's "Working with Gay Youth in Foster Care," Edward M. Roche's "Residential Care for Lesbian and Gay Adolescents," David Louis' "Peer Support Groups," Evelyn Poates' "Employment and Training Services for Homeless Sexual Minority Youth," George Belitsos' "Rural Gay and Lesbian Youth," A. Billy Jones' "The Need for Cultural Sensitivity in Working with Third World Lesbian and Gay Youth," and Marion Zimmer Bradley's "The Implications of Sex Role Conformity for Lesbian and Gay Youth."

750 Bullough, Vern L., W. Dorr Legg, Barrett W. Elcano, and James Kepner. An Annotated Bibliography of Homosexuality. New York: Garland Publishing, 1976.

Volume one includes entries on bibliography, general studies, behavioral sciences, education and children, medicine and biology, law and its enforcement, military, and religion and ethics. Volume two includes entries on biography and autobiography, studies (on literature and the arts), fiction, poetry, the homophile movement, periodicals, and transvestism and transsexualism.

751 Crawford, William. Homosexuality in Canada: A Bibliography. Toronto: Canadian Gay Archives, 1984.

Written in both English and French, the bibliography includes entries on art, book reviews, education, essays, pederasty, family life, gay liberation, Canadian gay periodicals, lesbian and feminist periodicals, lesbianism, history, sports, publishing, public opinion, politics, video, film, film reviews and articles on film, personalities and interviews, literature (anthologies), literature (autobiography and biography), literary criticism, unpublished literary criticism, literature (drama), literature (micellaneous), literature (poetry), literature (short stories), songs, sociology and anthropology, social work, alcoholism and drug addiction, medicine, sexology, medicine, medicine (AIDS), psychiatry and psychology, psychology in the popular press, prisons and criminology, police, law, law in the popular press, criminal cases, matrimonial cases, civil rights cases, cases involving transsexuals, civil rights and censorship, briefs and reports, government documents, religion, theses, miscellaneous materials, directories, cataloques, bibliographies and indexes, Canadian Gay Archives (vertical files), and Canadian Gay Archives (collection).

752 Crew, Louie, ed. The Gay Academic. Palm Springs: ETC Publications, 1978.

Crew begins "An Antidote to Hemlock," which serves as the introduction to the book, by writing that: "After over 2,000 years of being stigmatized as 'corrupters of youth,' gay academics are declaring themselves to be what they have always been, viz. an intregral part of the academy, serving with distinction in the academy's most celebrated achievements as well as in its more mundane endeavors, certainly with no demonstrable monopoly on corruption, sexual or otherwise." In The Gay Academic, lesbian and gay academics contribute articles on general academic issues, as well as from the disciplines of history, library science, linguistics, literature (criticism, general, American, English, French, and German), philosophy, psychology, religion and theology, science, and sociology and political science.

753 Cruikshank, Margaret, ed. Lesbian Studies: Present and Future. Old Westbury, NY: Feminist Press, 1982.

Lesbian Studies is a collection of essays organized under the following categories: "Lesbians in the Academic World: The Personal/Political Experience," "In the Classroom," "New Research/New Perspectives," and "Resources." An appendix includes a sample syllabus for a lesbian studies course. A bibliography of books and one on articles is also provided.

754 Dixon, V.J. and B.G Foster, eds. Beyond Black or White: An Alternative America. Boston: Little, Borwn, 1971.

The book includes W.E. Cross' "Discovering the Black Referent: The Psychology of Black Liberation" which gives some background on homosexuality in the black community.

755 Gonsiorek, John C., ed. A Guide to Psychotherapy with Gay and Lesbian Clients. New York: Harrington Park Press, 1985.

Originally published as the Journal of Homosexuality 7.2/3 (1981/82), the book includes the following essays. John C. Gonsiorek's "The Use of Diagnositic Concepts in Working with Gay and Lesbian Populations," "Martin Rochlin's "Sexual Orientation of the Therapist and Therapeutic Effectiveness with Gay Clients," Eli Coleman's "Developmental Stages of the Coming Out Process," Bronwyn D. Anthony's "Lesbian Client-Lesbian Therapist: Opportunities and Challenges in Working Together," Alan K. Malyon's "Psychotherapeutic Implications of Internalized Homophobia in Gay Men," Barbara M. McCandlish's "Therapeutic Issues with Lesbian Couples," David P. McWhirter and Andrew M. Mattison's "Psychotherapy for Gay Male Couples," Eli Coleman's "Bisexual and Gay Men in Heterosexual Marriage: Conflicts and Resolutions in Therapy," David Conlin and Jaime Smith's "Group Psychotherapy for Gay Men," Rex Reece's "Group Treatment of Sexual Dysfunction in Gay Men," Michael F. Myers's "Counseling the Parents of Young Homosexual Male

Patients," Craig Anderson's "Males as Sexual Assualt Victims: Multiple Levels of Trauma," James B. Nelson's "Religious and Moral Issues in Working with Homosexual Clients," William G. Herron, et al's "Psychoanalytic Psychotherapy for Homosexual Clients: New Concepts," and John C. Gonsiorek's "Organizational and Staff Problems in Gay/Lesbian Mental Health Agencies."

756 Grahn, Judy. Another Mother Tongue: Gay Words, Gay Worlds. Boston: Beacon Press,1984

Because there is no acceptance and exploration of homosexual slang words to enter the dictionary, Grahn takes an etymological approach to such words as "faggot," "fairy," "bulldike," and "lavender" to find what these words mean to gay men and lesbians. Doing so, she suggests "parameters and characteristics of homosexual culture as I have experienced it and as others have spoken or written about it. In doing so, I have often used stereotypes, even derogatory ones, very deliberately, as points of entry into the history, for something about stereotypes is usually true and therefore open to study." Anther Mother Tongue is not a dictionary. Instead, it is a collection of short essays, historical anecdotes, stories, poetry, and commentary.

757 Grier, Barbara. The Lesbian in Literature. Tallahasse, FL: Naiad Press, 1981.

Grier has compiled a list of books which have lesbian content "no matter how negative or slight." Books which have a major lesbian component are highlighted.

758 Moses, A. Elfin and Robert O. Hawkins, Jr. Counseling Lesbian Women and Gay Men: A Life-Issues Approach. St. Louis: The C.V. Mosby Company, 1982.

Counseling Lesbian Women and Gay Men is divided into four sections: how the world views gay people, gay experience, special issues in counseling gay clients, and a summation.

759 Parker, William. Homosexuality: A Selective Bibliography of Over 3,000 Items. Metuchen, NJ: Scarecrow Press, 1971.

Parker's bibliography includes entries organized under the following categories: books, pamphlets and documents, theses and dissertations, articles in books, newpaper articles, articles in popular magazines, articles in religious journals, articles in legal journals, court cases involving consenting adults, articles in medical and scientific journals, articles in other specialized journals, articles in homophile publications, literary works, and miscellaneous works (movies, television programs, and phonograph records). The following two supplements have also been published by Scarecrow Press: Homosexuality Bibliography: Supplement, 1970-1975 (1977), Homosexuality Bibliography: Second Supplement, 1976-1982 (1985).

760 Roberts, J.R. Black Lesbians: An Annotated Bibliogrpahy. Naiad Press, 1981.

The entries are organized under the following categories: "Lives and Lifestyles," "Oppression, Resistance, and Liberation," "Literature and Criticism," "Photographs," "Music and Musicians," "Periodicals," "Research, Reference, and Popular Studies," and "Addendum." An appendix includes materials relating to the "Norton Sound" case.

761 Rofes, Eric E. "I Thought People Like That Killed Themselves": Lesbians, Gay Men, and Suicide. San Francisco: Grey Fox Press, 1983.

Rofes includes chapters on "The Myth and Fact of Gay Suicide," "Scandal, Blackmail, and Public Exposure," "Lesbian and Gay Youth and Suicide," "Suicide and Activists," "Substance Abuse and Gay Suicide," "Areas for Continued Research," and "Ending Gay Suicide." In this text, "gay" denotes both men and women.

762 Schur, E.M. The Politics of Deviance: Stigma Contests and the Uses of Power. Englewood Cliffs, NJ: Prentice-Hall, 1980.

An investigation into the implications which arise from those who deviate from society's norms.

763 Weinberg, George. Society and the Healthy Homosexual. 1972. New York: St. Martin's Press, 1983.

Weinberg begins the preface to the 1972 edition with the comment that "The Prevailing attitude toward homosexuals in the US and many other countries is revulsion and hostility.....[D]iscriminatory practices against homosexuals have deep psychological motives." And it is these psychological motives which are investigated in Society and the Healthy Homosexual. Although he realizes that not all homosexuals are healthy individuals, Weinberg takes the position that it is not the the homosexuality per se that makes one unhealthy. But those who are unhealthy are outside the scope of this book. Instead, Weinberg examines the issue of homophobia, "an attitude held by many non-homosexuals and perhaps by the majority of homosexuals in countries where there is discrimination against homosexuals." He begins Society and the Healthy Homosexual with a chapter on homophobia followed by one which examines how homophobia causes a bias in psychoanalysis. The remaining chapters explore: the case against trying to convert, the healthy homosexual, communication with parents, words for the new culture, and the dread of being alone.

764 --- and Alan P. Bell. Homosexuality: An Annotated Bibliography. New York: Harper and Row, 1972.

The entries in this book are organized under the following categories: physiological considerations, psychological considerations, sociological considerations, and other bibliographies and dictionaries.

765 Young, Ian. The Male Homosexual in Literature: A Bibliography. Metuchen, NJ, 1975.

Young explains: "This bibliography is an alphabetical listing by author of English-language works of fiction, drama, poetry and autobiography concerned with male homosexuality or having male homosexual characters. Though an attempt has been made to include the most important works, the listing is selective and is not intended to be exhaustive." Also included in the bibliography are the following essays: Ian Young's "The Flower Beneath the Foot: A Short History of the Gay Novel," Graham Jackson's "The Theatre of Implications: Homosexuality in Drama," Ian Young's "The Poetry of Male Love," and Rictor Norton's "Ganymede Raped: Gay Literature--The Critic as Censor."

Lesbian and Gay Literature

766 Brady, Maureen. Folly. Trumansburg, NY: Crossing Press, 1982.

Folly concerns black and white working class women who organize a strike in a Carolina mill town. The women grow as they realize the realities of racism, heterosexism, and the economics of survival.

767 ---. Give Me Your Good Ear. Argyle, NY: Spinsters, Ink, 1979.

Violence, daily work, and female connections are the focus of Brady's novel. Give Me Your Good Ear allows the reader to experience a daughter's struggle to break the chain of mind binding and blindings which are passed from generation to generation.

768 Covina, Gina and Laurel Galana. The Lesbian Reader: An Amazon Quarterly Anthology. Berkeley: Amazon Press, 1975.

A collection of material which has appeared in the Amazon Quarterly, a lesbian literary journal.

769 Hoffman, William M. As Is. New York: Vintage Books, 1985.

Nominated for three Tony awards (including one for best play) and winner of the 1985 Drama Desk Award for outstanding new play, As Is focuses on the plight of an AIDS patient, his family, and his friends.

770 Isherwood, Christopher. A Single Man. 1964; New York: Avon, 1978.

The main character in A Single Man is George, a middle-aged homosexual who is attempting to come to terms with not only his aging but the recent death of his lover and his relationship to his neighbors, his students, and the heterosexual world. Typical of Isherwood's "I Am A Camera" style, the reader is allowed to follow George through one complete day.

771 Preston, John. Entertainment for a Master. Boston: Alyson Publications, 1986.

Entertainment for a Master is a well written novel with an S&M focus. Not only does all the sexual activity follow the safe-sex guidelines developed to lessen the chances of contracting AIDS, but Preston teaches his readers how to practice S&M safely. Instead of focusing on rape, abuse or drunken masters, and violence, the protagonist recognizes that the ritualized sex needs to be performed within the slave's limitations, that sexual activity is negotiated in advance, and that certain practices such as whipping the lower back (where the kidneys are located) can cause damage. And, more importantly, even though the protagonist drinks, he is a moderate drinker who realizes that alcohol and drugs interfere with sexual enjoyment and could lead to unsafe practices.

772 ---. Franny: The Queen of Provincetown. Boston: Alyson, 1985.

Franny is an ugly drag queen who makes her home in Provincetown. Each chapter in this book describes one of the men who have entered her life (usually as friends, sometimes as lovers). Each man who comes into contact with Franny has his life transformed from his trapped existance into a productive, happy individual. For example, a professor sobers up through AA and eventually writes the gay novel which has been collecting dust in his desk drawer. The characters in Franny cover the range of individuals found in the gay community: drag queens, leather men, artists, bartenders, professors, hustlers, individuals just accepting their sexuality, et cetera.

773 ---, ed. Hot Living: Erotic Stories About Safer Sex. Boston: Alyson, 1985.

A collection of short stories, Hot Living advocates that "Sex is not over with [because of the AIDS crisis]. There are ways to have sex that are enjoyable, and that are desirable." Preston recognizes the educational value of erotic fiction and he and the other contributors supply stories whose characters can serve as models for safe sex. Although the stories often become preachy, with only a little imagination on the reader's part, the activities described can easily be replicated or serve as the basis for masturbatory fantasy. The contributors to this collection represent some of the formost gay writers of erotica: John Preston, Phil Andros, Toby Johnson, George Whitmore, Tripp Vanderford, T.R. Witomski, Robin Metcalfe, Max Exander, Mach, Marty Rubin, Frank Mosca, Darrell Yates Rist, Eric Rofes, and David Barton-Jay.

774 Smith, Michael, ed. Black Men/White Men: A Gay Anthology. San Francisco: Gay Sunshine Press, 1983.

The anthology is a collection of short stories, poetry, testimonials, essays, and articles which record the experience of black and white men together. Photos and drawings are also included.

775 South, Cris. Clenched Fists, Burning Crosses: A Novel of Resistance. Trumansburg, NY: Crossing Press, 1984.

The novel concerns a group of lesbians who confront the Ku Klux Klan. Portions are violent.

776 Taylor, Valerie. Prism. Tallahassee, FL: Naiad, 1981.

Prism is a novel about a 60 year old woman who meets another elderly lesbian who is still closeted. These women discover that love, sex, and dreams are not just for the young.

777 Toder, Nancy. Choices: A Classic Lesbian Love Story. Boston: Alyson, 1980.

The joy, passion, conflicts, and intensity of love between women is the focus of Choices. Toder writes about the fear and confusion of a woman coming to terms with her attraction to other women.

778 Virga, Vincent. A Comfortable Corner. New York: Avon, 1982.

Virga writes a novel in which realistic treats the issue of alcoholism principally from the co-alcoholic's point of view. Besides watching Christopher More, the main character, learn to deal with his lover's alcoholism, the reader is able to see how he has integrated his sexuality into all areas of his life.

779 Warren, Patricia Nell. The Front Runner. 1974; New York: Bantam, 1977.

Although The Front Runner has been out of print for several years, if availiable, it is an excellent book for a newly self-accepting gay man. The story concerns a world champion runner and his coach/lover. However,

Billy Sive, "the front runner," is assassinated just before he crosses the Olympic finish line.

Journals and Periodicals Concerning Gay/Lesbian Issues

780 The Advocate, Liberation Publications, Inc., Box 4371, Los Angeles, CA 90078-4371.

The largest gay magazine in the country, The Advocate features news in the arts, politics, and religion. Each issue includes a feature article as well as book and movie reviews as are regular features on AIDS, newsbriefs, and personal ads. The focus is primarily white, upwardly mobile gay men. The Advocate is published bi-weekly.

781 The Baltimore Gay People, 241 W. Chase Street, Baltimore, MY 21203.

The paper serves the lesbian/gay community of the Baltimore area.

782 Bay Windows, 1515 Washington Street, Boston, MA 02118.

Bay Windows bills itself as "New England's Largest Gay and Lesbian Newspaper" and it takes seriously that its audience is both gay men and lesbians. It is published weekly.

783 Body Politic, Box 7289, Station A, Toronto, Ontario M5W 1X9 CANADA.

As we were going to press, we leared that The Body Politic is no longer being published.

784 Capitol Hill, Gay Rights National Lobby, 1606 17th Street, NW, Washington, DC 20009.

Capitol Hill is the monthly newsletter of the Gay

Rights National Lobby and features news on national legislative issues that affect gay men and lesbians.

785 Christopher Street, That New Magazine, Inc., Suite 417, 250 West 57th Street, New York, NY 10019.

Published monthly, Christopher Street features articles of interest to gay men. Book and movie reviews are a regular feature and the magazine is especially noted for its cartoons.

786 Common Lives/Lesbian Lives, Box 1553, Iowa City, IA 52244.

A quarterly publication featuring stories, journals, graphics, essays, humor, poetry, and autobiography. Common Lives/Lesbian Lives is committed to insure access to women whose lives have traditionally been denied visibility and to encourage women who have never published to do so.

787 The Evergreen Chronicles: A Regional Journal of Gay and Lesbian Writers, Box 6260, Minnehaha Station, Minneapolis, MN 55406.

Published quarterly, The Evergreen Chronicles draws its artistic talents from the North Dakota, South Dakota, Wisconsin, Minnesota, Kansas, Missouri, Nebraska, Ohio, Illinois, Indiana, and Michigan Region. All submissions should be copies, not originals. A self-addressed stamped envelope is required to have submission returned. Prose should be no more than fifteen double spaced pages. Poetry should be single spaced. Black and white graphics are also welcomed.

788 Gay and Lesbian Press Association Newsletter, Box 7809, Van Nuys, CA 91409.

The newsletter is published quarterly and features material which interests individuals working with the lesbian/gay press.

789 Gay Community News, 67 Berkeley Street, Boston, MA 02116.

A monthly publication for the lesbian and gay community, Gay Community News give national and New England news relevant to both lesbians and gay men. It has a distinct New England flavor.

790 The Gay News-Telegraph, Piasa Publishing Company, 10 S. Euclid Avenue, St. Louis, MO 63108.

Published monthly, the paper is focused on "serving gay men and Lesbians in the heart of America": Arkansas, Missouri, Illinois, Kentucky, and Tennessee.

791 IGLA Bulletin, International Gay and Lesbian Archives, 1654 N. Hudson Ave., Hollywood, CA 90028.

The IGLA Bulletin features articles which would interest those people who are interested in lesbian/gay history and literature.

792 Insight: A Quarterly of Lesbian/Gay Christian Opinion, Box 5110, Grand Central Station, New York, NY 10163.

Insight's board of advisors and content reflect a healthy ecumenical approach to the Christian tradition. The focus of the journal is to enlighten the non-homosexual community and to advance the ministries of the lesbian and gay Christian community.

793 Into the Courts, National Gay Rights Advocates, 540 Castro Street, San Francisco, CA 94114.

The newsletter of the National Gay Rights Advocates, Into the Courts features information on court cases that impact the lesbian/gay community.

794 Journal of Homosexuality, Haworth Press, 28 E. 22nd Street, New York, NY 10010.

The Journal of Homosexuality is a quarterly journal which allows scholars to publish research concerning lesbian and gay issues. Sometimes, an issue will focus around a particular theme.

795 Lesbian Connection, Ambitious Amazons, Box 811, East Lansing, MI 48823.

A reader written journal of national importance, The Lesbian Connection allows lesbians to share thoughts on various political, social, cultural, and religious issues. It has often been especially helpful to lesbian women who live in isolation from other lesbians.

796 Lesbian Ethics, Box 943, Venice, CA 90294.

Published three times a year, Lesbian Ethics provides a forum for lesbians to talk about their values and beliefs.

797 New York Native, 281 W. Broadway, New York, NY 10013.

A weekly publication of the lesbian and gay community, The New York Native includes national and international news items. Special focus is given to New York City events. Feature articles appear in each issue as do columns on such things as film, dance, records, and travel.

798 PWA Coalition Newsline, 263A West 19th Street, Room 125, New York, NY 10011.

The Newsline is by, for, and about people with AIDS and ARC. The insights and experiences shared by PWA's and their friends in the Newline impact how individuals view AIDS and ARC. They also force the reader to take a hard look at the what's, the why's, and the how's of the medical, political, and social challenges in which the lesbian/gay community is engaged.

799 RFD: A Country Journal for Gay Men Everywhere, Running Water, Rte. #1, Box 127-E, Bakersville, NC 28705.

Published quarterly, RFD is "a reader-written journal for gay men which focuses on country living and encourages alternative lifestyles. Articles often explore the building of a sense of community, radical faerie consciousness, the caring for the environment, as well as sharing gay men's experiences." Features include book reviews, brothers behind bars, contact letters, country kitchen, fey arts, fiction, health, poetry, politics, and spirituality. Issues frequently have a section featuring articles based on a particular topic.

800 The Weekly News, 901 N.E. 79th Street, Miami, FL 33138.

A newspaper which features news of interest to the Florida lesbian/gay community.

801 Update, Box 7762, San Diego, CA 92107.

A lesbian/gay newspaper that features news from Southern California.

802 The Works, Berg Investment Corporation, 303 N. Senate Ave., Indianapolis, IN 46204.

Published monthly, The Works provides brief news articles of interest to gay men and lesbians with special focus on Indiana and the surrounding area. Periodically, feature articles also appear.

Mail Order Book Stores

803 Chosen Books, 940 W. McNichols, Detroit, MI 48203.

Send a 3' x 5' card with your name and address to receive their catalogue.

804 Giovanni's Room, 1145 Pine Street, Philadelphia, PA 19107.

To obtain a catalogue, phone their toll free number, 1-800-222-6996. Once on the mailing list, you will receive the catalogue as well as supplements directed either to the gay or lesbian reader.

805 Lambda Rising, 2012 S Street, NW, Washington, DC 20009.

Lambda Rising publishes _The Whole Gay Catalog: Books for Gay Men and Lesbians, Their Family and Friends_. To obtain a copy, phone 1-800-621-6969.

806 Oscar Wilde Memorial Bookstore, 15 Christopher Street, New York, NY 10014.

The Oscar Wilde Memorial Bookstore publishes a mail order catalogue. Their phone number is 212-255-8097.

SELECTED BIBLIOGRAPHY ON

ALCOHOLISM AND SUBSTANCE ABUSE

Between 24-40% of the lesbian and gay community is alcohol or drug dependent. Although more and more lesbians and gay men are working to address this major health problem, often, individuals do not know where to get good information of alcoholism and substance abuse. The following section of the _NALGAP Annotated Bibliography_ lists some of the best and most available references for individuals interested in learning more about chemical addiction.

General Information on Chemical Addiction

807 Bissell, LeClair and Paul W. Haberman. _Alcoholism in the Professions_. New York: Oxford University Press 1984.

The book permits the comparison of the experiences of alcoholics in five different professions: attorneys, physicians, nurses, dentists, and social workers. Written in two parts, first the methodology of the study and the results of interviews and follow-up interviews is recorded. The second section, "Addressing the Problem," includes information on the professional as a member of AA, the organizational response of professionals in the study, the response of other professionals, and recommendations for action. Of particular value is an 18 page summary of the findings which helps the reader identify the highlights in each section of the book.

809 Brown, Stephanie. _Treating the Alcoholic: A_

Developmental Model of Recovery. New York: John Wiley and Sons, 1985.

In Treating the Alcoholic, Brown proposes a model of treatment that combines Alcoholics Anonymous and psychotherapy. As she explains in the preface: "It is a book that merges theory and practice from diverse schools of psychology with the concrete experience of AA members." Part of her purpose is to help improve communication between the alcoholic (both those who are drinking and those who are in recovery) and the helping professionals. After explaining the model, she decribes its clinical application and the relationship between AA and psychotherapy. Family issues are also addressed.

810 Gitlow, Stanley and H.S. Peyser. Alcoholism: A Practical Treatment Guide. New York: Grune and Stratton, 1980.

Although the primary audience for the book is medical doctors, it is also and excellent resource for other professionals.

811 Johnson, Vernon E. I'll Quit Tomorrow. New York: Harper and Row, 1973.

I'll Quit Tomorrow is based on the belief that alcoholics "had suffered a build-up of crises that brought them to a recognition of their condition. The crises themselves were usually fortuitiously grouped together so that they broke through the almost impenetrable defenses of the victims of the disease, which were organized into highly efficient 'denial systems.'" The text addresses such issues as the drinking culture in which we live, the rising cost of dependency, rational defenses and projection, blackouts, repression, euphoric recall, the dynamics of intervention, the cry for help and the use of crisis, treatment of the acute phase, characterological conflict, the stages of recovery, rehabilitation, counseling alcoholics, and the dynamics of forgiveness. Appendixes include handbooks for patients, outpatients, hospital personnel, and the clergy. Evaluations and suggestions for "first step" preparation are also included.

812 ---. Intervention: How to Help Someone Who Doesn't Want Help, A Step-by-Step Guide for Families and Friends of Chemically Dependent Persons. Minneapolis: Johnson Institute Books, 1986.

Unlike most books about helping individuals who are chemically dependent, Intervention advances the theory that someone doesn't have to wait until the chemically dependent person in their life "hits bottom." As Johnson writes in the preface: "Waiting is too dangerous. It is also cruel. It allows an already bad situation to get worse....You can reach out now." The first part of the book discusses chemical dependency. Then, in the second section, "Intervening with Chemical Dependency," the reader is taught how to prepare for an intervention and how to do an intervention.

813 Kurtz, Ernest. Shame and Guilt: Charateristics of the Dependency Cycle (An Historical Perspective for Professionals). Center City, MN: Hazelden Foundation, 1981.

Kurtz makes a distinction between the experience of shame and the experience of guilt as they relate to the alcoholic or chemically dependent person.

814 Lender, Mark Edward and James Kirby Martin. Drinking in America: A History. New York: Free Press, 1982.

Lender and Martin give an in-depth analysis of the role which drinking has played in America from the colonial period to the present.

815 Moore, Jean, ed. Roads to Recovery: A National Directory of Alcohol and Drug Addiction Treatment

Centers. New York: Macmillan Publishing Company, 1985.

Treatment centers are listed by state under the following headings, "Eastern Treatment Centers," "Central/Southern Treatment Centers," and "Western Treatment Centers." Appendices include national associations, organizations, and government agencies as well as state alcohol and drug agencies. Treatment centers for the following groups are indexed: adolescents, blacks, gays/lesbians, hearing impaired/deaf, hispanic, impaired physicians and health professionals, men only, native Americans, older adults, priests, nuns, brothers, women only, and retreat centers for addiction workers.

816 Page, Penny Booth. Alcohol Use and Alcoholism: A Guide to the Literature. New York: Garland Publishing, 1986.

A very good bibliography by the Rutger's librarian.

817 Rudy, David. Becoming Alcoholic: Alcoholics Anonymous and the Reality of Alcoholism. Carbondale: Southern Illinois University Press, 1986.

Rudy's emphasis is how an alcoholic becomes an "AA alcoholic," someone who adopts the world view of Alcoholic's Anonymous. A non-alcoholic himself, Rudy's book is based on 18 months of field work in "Mideastern City, USA" where he attended both open and closed meetings of AA, met people at a local Alano Club, and interviewed AA alcoholics about their drinking, recovery, and world view. In Becoming Alcoholic, Rudy explains such issues as various perspectives on AA, the process of affiliation with AA, the types of drinkers who affiliate with AA, slipping and sobriety, and alcoholic worlds and sociological worlds.

818 Spickard, Anderson and Barbara R. Thompson. Dying for a Drink: What You Should Know About Alcoholism. Waco, TX: Word Books, 1985.

Spickard and Thompson look at alcoholism from a Christian point of view. However, they take the realistic view that belief in God is not sufficient for recovery. The alcoholic must take certain steps in order for recovery to take place. Suggestions are given to family members and ministers who wish to help the alcoholic.

819 Strachan, J. George. Alcoholism: Treatable Illness. Vancouver, BC: Mitchell Press Limited, 1968.

Strachan's comprehensive book is organized into three sections: the nature and magnitude of the illness, the illness concept, and treating the illness.

Twelve Step Programs

820 Al-Anon Faces Alcoholism. 1965; New York: Al-Anon Family Group Headquarters, 1985.

Al-Anon Faces Alcoholism approaches the problem of alcoholism from three different perspectives. First, those who work with the problem of alcoholism describe what can be done to help the alcoholic. Second, those who live with the problem of alcoholism tell their stories. Finally, the nature of Al-Anon is described, the steps and traditions of the program are described, and the tools of the program (slogans, serenity prayer, sponsorship, and conference approved literature) are explained.

821 Al-Anon's Twelve Steps and Twelve Traditions. 1981; New York: Al-Anon Family Group Headquarters, 1983.

The twelve steps and twelve traditions of the Al-Anon Program are explained. Each explanation is followed by a reflection which helps the individual understand how the step can be used in their situation and a story about how the step worked in an Al-Anon's member's life.

822 *Alcoholics Anonymous: The Story of How Many Thousands of Men and Women Have Recovered from Alcoholism.* 1939; New York: Alcoholics Anonymous World Services, 1976.

Typically referred to as "the big book," *Alcoholics Anonymous* discusses alcoholism, the AA program, and how the program can work in peoples' lives. The book ends with the personal stories of AA members.

823 *Came to Believe...: The Spiritual Adventure of AA as Experienced by Individual Members.* New York: Alcoholics Anonymous World Services, 1973.

AA is a spiritual way of life. In the forward, the editors write that *Came to Believe*... "is designed as an outlet for the rich diversity of convictions implied in 'God *as we understood Him*.'" Contributors discuss the general issue of spirituality as well as spiritual experiences, prayer, release from obsession, spiritual awakening, the search, coincidence, a higher power, spiritual progress, and "in all our affairs."

824 Kurtz, Ernest. *Not-God: A History of Alcoholics Anonymous.* Center City, MN: Hazelden, 1979.

In *Not God*, Kurtz first gives a history of AA's development. Then, he discusses the implications of AA's spirituality by placing the movement in the larger context of American history and the history of religious ideas. Finally, he talks about the meaning and significance of AA's understanding of spirituality/religion.

825 *Living Sober: Some Methods AA Members Have Used for Not Drinking.* New York: Alcoholics Anonymous World Services, 1975.

Living Sober was edited by Barry L., a gay man who is a recovering alcoholic. As he explains in the first section: "This booklet does *not* offer a plan for recovery from alcoholism....Here, we tell only some methods we have used for living *without* drinking."

826 Twelve Steps and Twelve Traditions. New York: Alcoholics Anonymous World Services, 1952.

The book explains the twelve steps and traditions used in the program of Alcoholics Anonymous.

Women and Substance Abuse

827 Eddy, Cristen C. and John L. Ford, eds. Alcoholism in Women. Dubuque, IA: Kendall/Hunt, 1980.

The book examines the broad spectrum of recent study in the field of alcoholism. The essays which are included are grouped under the following headings: "Etiological Factors," "Primary and Secondary Prevention," and "Treatment."

828 Kirkpatrick, Jean. Turnabout: New Help for the Woman Alcoholic. 1978. Seattle: Madrona, 1986.

The Women for Sobriety Program, founded by Kirkpatrick is introduced in this book. Women for Sobriety is a 13 step program designed around the specific needs of women.

829 Norwood, Robin. Women Who Love Too Much: When You Keep Wishing and Hoping He'll Change. New York: Jeremy P. Tarcher, Inc., 1985.

While not specifically a book about substance abuse, Norwood's explanation of the lessons learned in dysfunctional families often involve examples of dependency and co-dependency. Not only are patterns explained, but suggestions are given on how to break unhealthy ways of behaving. Although the book is addressed specifically to a female audience, it is very applicable to men who suffer from/in unhealthy relationships.

830 Sandmaier, Marian. The Invisible Alcoholics: Women and Alcohol Abuse in America. New York: McGraw-Hill, 1980.

Sandmaier writes in the introduction: "This book is an attempt to give the alcoholic woman the identity that has always been denied her. It aims first of all to simply bring her into the light of our consciousness, so that her existence and her pain can no longer be misread or ignored, But equally important, it tries to record and interpret women's actual experience in the grip of alcohol." Chapters in the book include, the scope of the problem, the making of an alcoholic woman, housewives, employed women, minority women, teenage girls, lesbians, women on skid row, and the hazards of treatment.

831 Swallow, Jean, ed. Out from Under: Sober Dykes and Our Friends. San Francisco: Spinsters, Ink, 1983.

Stories, poetry, essays, and interviews about recovery in the lesbian community.

832 V., Rachel. A Women Like You: Life Stories of Women Recovering from Alcoholism and Addiction. San Francisco: Harper and Row, 1985.

Rachel V. records the stories of 19 women who have sobered up in Alcoholics Anonymous.

833 Wilsnack, Sharon C. and Linda J. Beckwith, eds. Alcohol Problems in Women: Antecedents, Consequences, and Intervention. New York: Guilford Press, 1984.

The essays collected in this book are grouped under the following categories: "Patterns of Alcohol Use and Alcohol Problems in Women," "Antecedents and Consequences of Alcohol Problems in Women," and "Female Alcohol Abuse: Its Effects on the Family."

Children and Chemical Addiction

834 Ackerman, Robert J. Children of Alcoholics: A Guidebook for Educators, Therapists, and Parents. 1979. Holmes Beach, FL: Learning Publications, 1983.

Ackerman describes what it's like to be a child of an alcoholic. He then offers suggestions to parents, educators, and therapists who wish to help children in an alcoholic situation.

835 Black, Claudia. It Will Never Happen to Me. Denver: MAC, 1982.

In her introduction, Black explains that: "While children of alcoholics are at high risk to become alcoholic, research also demonstrates children of alcoholics are often prone to marry those who are, or become alcoholic. In addition...should a child of an alcoholic neither become alcoholic, nor marry an alcoholic, emotional and/or psychological patterns develop which may cause problems in this person in adulthood." The book explains how roles and behaviors learned in a dysfunctional family cause dysfunctional activity to be passed from the alcoholic to the child of the alcoholic.

836 Bissell, LeClair and Richard Weatherwax. The Cat Who Drank Too Much. Bantam, CT: Bibulophile Press, 1984.

Bissell and Weatherwax combine photographs and simple text to tell the story of an alcoholic cat. Good for children as well as adults, the book is also available in Spanish.

837 Deutsch, Charles. Broken Bottles, Broken Dreams: Understanding and Helping the Children of Alcoholics. New York: Teachers College Press, 1982.

The text is concerned with the millions of school-age

children who suffer from the impact of alcoholism. Subjects covered range from the characteristics of the alcoholic family, the child's reaction to the family system, children's views of drinking, and ways in which to help the child from an alcoholic family.

Journals

838 Alcoholism and Addiction, Box 31329, Seattle, WA 98103.

Published six times a year, Alcoholism and Addiction is written for treatment professionals, recovering alcoholics and chemically dependent people, family members seeking information about alcoholism and addiction, health care workers, concerned clergy, educations, and the general public. The editors are interested in short articles illustrating the principles of recovery as well as tips on living sober (e.g. tips on planning a sober vacation). Humor and short poetry are also welcome. Manuscripts should be typewritten and double-spaced and up to 2,500 words. Name, address, phone number, and working title should be included with each submission.

839 Changes, c/o U.S. Journal, Inc., 1721 Blount Road, Suite 1, Pompano Beach, FL 33069.

A bi-monthly magazine for children of alcoholics, Changes features prose, poetry, and songs written by children of alcoholics as well as capsule reviews of new developments and notable contributions in the field of alcoholism.

840 The Journal, 33 Russell Street, Toronto, CA M5S 2S1.

A monthly publication of the Addiction Research Foundation of Ontario, The Journal publishes articles that are news stories about major developments in, or interesting aspects of, the field of alcohol and drug addicion. Because of its wide-spread audience, "local" items are avoided. Articles are 700-800 words although features can go up to 1,500 to 2,000 words. Deadline for stories in the first week of each month for the next month's issues. The Journal pays authors upon publication.

841 Journal of Studies on Alcohol, Box 969, Piscataway, NJ 08854.

Published six times a year, the Journal of Studies on Alcohol is a refereed journal which includes essays on general knowledge about alcohol, the use and misuse of alcohol, and alcoholic biomedical, behavioral, and socio-cultural effects.

842 NALGAP Newsletter, 1208 E. State Blvd., Fort Wayne, IN 46805.

The quarterly publication of the National Association of Lesbian and Gay Alcoholism Professionals, the NALGAP Newsletter provides not only membership information but articles, reviews, and highlights of developments in the field of substance abuse. It is available with membership in NALGAP.

843 Newservice, Box 5115, Phoenix, AZ 85010.

Newservice is an alternative magazine on behavior, health, and current events published by the Do It Now Foundation. The style for articles is to be authoriative and readable and should include frequent quotes. Newservice pays authors upon publication and suggests that potential contributors query first.

844 The U.S. Journal of Drug and Alcohol Dependence, 1721 Blout Road, Suite 1, Pompano Beach, FL 33069.

Billed as "the trade magazine for alcohol and drug professionals," The Journal is published monthly.

Catalogues

845 CompCare Publications, 2415 Annapolis Lane, Minneapolis, MN 55441.

CompCare's catelogue may be obtained by calling 1-800-328-3330.

846 Center of Alcohol Studies, Rutgers University, Box 969, Piscataway, NJ 08854.

A listing of books dealing with various issues in the alcoholism field.

847 Hazelden, Pleasant Valley Road, Box 176, Center City, MN 55012-0176.

Hazelden not only distributes the books that they publish but also substance abuse materials from other publishers as well as conference approved literature from AA, Al-Anon, NA, and OA. Their catalogue may be obtained by calling 612-257-4010 or 1-800-328-9000 (Continental United States). Minnesota residents may phone 1-800-257-0070.

848 Health Communications Catalog, 2119-A Hollywood Boulevard, Hollywood, FL 33020,

Published by the U.S. Journal, the catelogue lists books and pamphlets relevant to the field of chemical addiction.

849 National Council on Alcoholism, 12 West 21st Street, New York, NY 10010.

The National Council on Alcoholism publishes a catalogue of books, pamphlets, and reprints which they update yearly.

850 Wisconsin Clearinghouse, University of Wisconsin, Dean of Students Office, Dept. K, Box 1468, Madison, WI 53701.

The Wisconsin Clearinghouse's catelogue includes publications, posters, and tapes related to the field of chemical dependency.

ADDENDUM

Resources on Alcoholism, Substance Abuse, and Lesbians/Gay Men

851 "ACOAs and Homosexuality: What's the Connection?" Changes 1.6 (1987): 18+.

This article is an interview with Ellen Ratner, President of Pride Institute. In it, Ratner describes the work at Pride Institute, a 36 bed treatment center devoted exclusively to lesbians and gay men. The interview was conducted by Debbie Hazelton.

852 B., Laird. "Of Course, I Go to Regular Meetings Too." Newsletters Anonymous 1 (1986): 5.

Laird discusses the need to go to non-lesbian/gay meetings of AA as well as lesbian/gay ones.

853 ---. "What Gives?" Newsletters Anonymous 2 (1987): 1.

A general discussion of Lambda Services Group and the services which they provide to the sober lesbian/gay community.

854 B., M. "Risking the Truth." Box 1980 ["The Grapevine"] 43.9 (1987); 31-3.

M. B., a gay alcoholic who recovered through Alcoholics Anonymous, discusses the issue of honesty as it relates to his sexuality.

855 B., Thommie. "How Soon We Forget." Newsletters Anonymous 1 (1986): 2.

Thommie, a black gay alcoholic, discusses homophobia both within American culture, the gay community, and AA.

856 Berg, Steven L. "Drunks Make Poor Revolutionaries." NALGAP News 7.1 (1986): 9-10.

A modified version of the article of the same name which appeared in the Agenda.

857 ---. "Responding to Alcoholism." Dignity, Inc. Newsletter 18.8 (1986): 6.

Berg gives seven guidelines as to how individuals in the lesbian/gay community can better respond to alcoholism within the community.

858 ---. Rev. Alcoholism in the Professions. by LeClair Bissell and Paul Haberman. NALGAP News 7.2/3 (1987): in press.

Berg is favorably impressed with this book. Homosexuality is not specifically addressed.

859 ---. Rev. The Gentleman from Virginia. by Robert Bauman. NALGAP News 7.4 (1987): in press.

Berg concludes that because of his homophobia and the fact that he is unable to accept his past, Bauman's experiences are unable to help other recovering alcoholics come to terms with their addiction.

860 C., Doug. "Alcoholics Anonymous." tape. nd.

Doug C., a gay recovering alcoholic, reading the "Big Book."

861 Carvolth, James E. "Alcoholism in the Gay Community: An Overview and Treatment Approach." 1986. unpublished.

Carvolth first gives a general discussion of the role alcohol and bars play in the homosexual community. He then suggests how counselors can effectively treat gay/lesbian clients.

862 Cory, Donald Webster. The Homosexual in America. New York: Castle Books, 1951.

Cory accounts for the fact that most homosexuals are drug addicts or alcoholics because these people have never had contact with "normal homosexuals" who never had need for a counselor.

863 Covey, Ron. "IV Drug Abuse and AIDS: What Counselors Need to Know." Professional Counselor 1.3 (1986): 37-39+.

Covey explains how drug abuse is a co-factor in the development of AIDS. Suggestions are made as to how the substance abuse counselor can address this situation.

864 D., Pat. Rev. Gay and Sober. ed. Thomas O. Ziebold and John E. Mongeon. Newsletters Anonynmous 1 (1986): 2.

Pat summarizes each article in the book.

865 D., Ron. "Will You Be My Sponsor?" Newsletters Anonymous 1 (1986): 3.

A general discussion of AA sponsorship.

866 E., Eleanor. "Eleanor E." A Woman Like You. ed. Rachel V. Cambridge: Harper and Row, 1985. 155-67.

Eleanor tells the story of her alcoholism and recovery through AA. Her lover was also an alcoholic who recovered through AA and attended Al-Anon meetings as well.

867 E., Mike. "Hello Out There!" Newsletters Anonymous 1 (1986): 6.

Mike describes the services offered by the Lambda Services Group.

868 ---. "Reflections on the 1986 Gay/Lesbian Horizons Annual Conference, Evanston, Illinois." Newsletters Anonymous 2 (1987): 6-8.

A general overview of the conference.

869 Ellis, Edwin E. "Adult Children of Alcoholics." NALGAP News 8.1 (1986): 3.

Based on Janet Geringer Woititz's Adult Children of Alcoholics, Ellis explains characteristics of lesbian/gay ACOAs.

870 Faltz, Barbara G. and Scott Madover. "AIDS and Substance Abuse." Working with AIDS. ed. Michael Helquist. San Francisco: University of California, 1987. 162-79.

Faltz and Madover present strategies for coping with the clinical, ethical, and personal concerns of mental and medical health professionals working with persons with AIDS who are alcohol/drug dependent. In this articles are two case studies of white, gay men; one of whom is single the other who has a lover. Issues in working with codependent gay family relationships are described.

871 ---. "Substance Abuse as a Cofactor for AIDS." What to do About AIDS. ed. Leon McKusick. Berkeley: University of California Press, 1986. 154-62.

Faltz and Madover describe five ways in which substance abuse is linked to AIDS: direct transmission through sharing drug paraphinalia, transmission of the virus from IV drug users to their sex partners, infected women can transmit the virus during the neonatal period, use of immunosuppressant drugs such as poppers, and increased sexual and needle-using behavior while under the influence of drugs or alcohol.

872 Grotke, Mark. "Alcoholism: The Other Epidemic That's Destroying Gay Lives." The Advocate 446 (1986).

The author discusses the problem of alcoholism in the gay community.

873 Harte, K. Lorain. Rev. Dual Identities. by Dana Finnegan and Emily McNally. NALGAP News 8.2/3 (1987): in press.

Harte is especially impressed with the discussion of sexuality which is found in Dual Identities.

874 Helquist, Michael, ed. Working with AIDS: A Resource Guide for Mental Health Professionals. San Francisco: University of California, 1987.

This book includes Barbara Faltz's "AIDS and Substance Abuse."

875 Israelstam, Stephen. "Highlights from Survey of Opinions of Lesbians and Gay Alcoholism Professionals." NALGAP News 8.1 (1986): 11

The title is self explanatory.

876 Kahn, Samuel. Mentality and Homosexuality. Boston: Meddor Publishing, 1937.

Kahn writes that "most homosexuals are drug addicts, but most drug addicts are not homosexuals. As a rule the male and female homosexuals begin their addiction either at twenty years of age or before."

877 Kajdan, Bob. "New Beginnings." Reactions.

"New Beginnings" was a column on alcoholism in the lesbian/gay community which appeared in Reactions, from April 1986-December 1986.

878 Kus, Robert J. "Sobriety and the Quality of Life: Perceptions of Gay American Men." International

Conference on Alcohol Related Problems. Liverpool, England. April 9, 1987.

The paper is to shows how gay American men of AA evaluate the effects of sobriety on various aspects of their lives.

879 Liberacki, Alex. Rev. Invisible Wounds by Shelly Neiderback. NALGAP News 8.2/3 (1987): in press.

Liberacki's review is mostly favorable. Homosexuality nor chemical addiction is specifically addressed.

880 ---. Rev. From Grounded Theory to Clinical Practice. Ed. Carol W. Chenitz and Janice M. Swanson. NALGAP News 8.2/3 (1987): in press.

Liberacki focuses his comments on Robert Kuss' "From Grounded Theory to Clinical Practice."

881 McKusick, Leon. What to Do About AIDS: Physcians and Mental Health Professionals Discuss Issues. Berkeley: University of California Press, 1986.

This book includes Barbara Faltz's "Substance Abuse as a Co-Factor for AIDS."

882 ---. "Newsbriefs: Portland, OR." The Advocate 461 (1986): 27.

A brief article about the Right Step Recovery Program, a treatment facility for lesbian and gay men.

883 Newsletters Anonymous. Chicago: Lambda Service Group.

A bi-monthly publication serving the interests of the sober lesbian/gay community. Ordering information may be obtained by writing to the Lambda Service Group, 606 W. Barry, Box 231, Chicago, IL 60657.

884 Noble, Elaine. "The Political Agenda for Lesbians and

Gay Men in the 80s." Michigan State University, April 1986.

In this lecture, which is available only on tape, Noble, in part discusses her own alcoholism and recovery.

885 Phelps, D. Gary. "Getting Honest." New York Times Magazine 15 March 1987. sec. 6, p. 53.

In describing the neccesity of "getting honest," Phelps, a gay alcoholic, uses his own divorce and current relationship with another gay, divorced man as a case study.

876 Pohl, Mel. Letter. NALGAP News 8.1 (1986): 4.

A letter from Italy describing the first International Conference on Homosexuals and safe sex in Amsterdam and Florence.

887 "Pot Makes you Gay." The Works 6.4 (1987): 21.

The article is based on a Newsweek interview with Cariton Turner, drug advisor to the White House, who claims that marijuana makes you gay. We have been unable to locate the original Newsweek article.

888 "'Right Step' Gay/Lesbian Program Open." Professional Counselor 1.4 (1987): 45+.

A description of Christopher Eskeli, director of Right Step Recovery Program, a 32 bed unit featuring a predominantly gay/lesbian management, staff, and treatment plan.

889 Rist, Darrell Yates. "Bauman: The Man Behind the Sex Scandal." The Advocate 567 (1987): 37-9+.

Based on an interview with Bauman, Yates describes the former Congressman's career, downfall, and present life.

890 Ryan, Caitlin and Mel Pohl. Protocol for AIDS Education and Risk Reduction Counseling in Chemical Dependency Treatment Settings. Waltham: ARC Research Foundation, 1987.

In this booklet, Ryan and Pohl cover such topics as basic AIDS information, safe sex guidelines, AIDS and chemical dependency, HIV anti-body test, confidentiality, and HIV counseling.

891 Ryan, Virginia, ed. Effective Substance Abuse Counseling with Specific Population Groups. Lansing: Office of Substance Abuse Services, Michigan Department of Public Health, 1986.

The book includes a section on working with homosexual clients.

892 S., Jack. "Interview with Jim K." Newsletters Anonymous 2 (1987): 3-5.

Jim K. has been sober since 1965. In this interview, while summarizing his talk from the 1986 Chicago Roundup. He focuses on the homophobia of homosexual alcoholics.

893 S., Randy. "'Congrats,' Chicago '86." Newsletters Anonymous 1 (1986): 5.

Randy highlights the history of behind the first Chicago Lesbian/Gay Roundup.

894 Swallow, Jean. Leave a Light on for Me. San Francisco: Spinsters/Aunt Lute, 1986.

The novel includes an alcoholic lesbian with six years of recovery who comes from an alcoholic family.

895 Take a Step in the Right Direction. Portland: First Step Recovery Program, [1987].

A discussion of the services offered at Right Step, a chemical dependency treatment program designed around the needs of lesbians and gay men. Further information is available by writing 17645 NW St. Helens Road, Portland, OR 97231.

896 Taylor, Nancy. "Community Development as a Primary Network in Prevention of Alcohol Abuse Among Lesbians and Gay Men. Los Angeles: Alcoholism Center for Women, nd.

Taylor cites research that shows that "communities which have an acceptance of heavy alcohol use and an acceptance of drunkeness tend to have higher rates of alcohol abuse and alcoholism." As such, community development is crucial in "combatting the danger in denial and exercised through alcohol use as a coping tool and to include community-wide alcohol education while introducing new stress coping strategies."

897 Warren, Carol A.B. Identity and Community in the Gay World. New York: John Wiley and Sons, 1974.

Alcohol use and alcoholism are discussed throughout the book.

898 White, Bradford G. "Murder, She Read." Observation Balloon 21.2 (1987): 1-4

A case study of Bob Rogers, a gay alcoholic who murdered Goldie Levinstein, his wife.

899 Williams, Tennessee. Memoirs. Garden City: Doubleday, 1975.

Throughout the biography, Williams discusses his addiction to alcohol and other drugs.

900 Witomski, T.R. "Alcoholism." The Advocate 448 (1986): 6.

Witomski writes to compliment Mark Grotke's "Alcoholism." He emphasizes that alcoholism is a more serious disease in the gay community than is AIDS. The author is a recovering alcoholic.

901 ---. "Gay Bars, Gay Identities." Gay Life: Leisure, Love, and Living for the Contempory Gay Male. ed. Eric Rofes. Garden City: Dolphin, 1986. 201-09.

In this general discussion of gay bars, Witomski writes: "Because much gay socializing takes place in bars or at other gatherings where alcohol is available, and since homosexuals are bombarded daily with messages for the hetero world that tell them that being gay is not OK, alcoholism is pandemic among gay men."

902 World Directory of Gay/Lesbian Groups of Alcoholics Anonymous 1986-87. New York: International Advisory Council, 1986.

Copies of the directory may be obtained by writing to the International Advisory Council, Box 492, Village Station, New York, NY 10014.

Resources on

Alcoholism, Substance Abuse, or Homosexuality

903 Booth, Leo. Walking On Water: Life After Addiction. Pompano Beach, FL: Health Communications, 1985.

Fr. Booth, an Episcopal priest, offers his thoughts on developing a spiritual life that is compatable with twelve step programs.

904 Epicene, Lambda Resources, Box 460, Station A, Toronto, Ontario, M5M 2S9, Canada.

A new Canadian magazine for the lesbian and gay

community covering political and cultural events. It also acts as a forum for gay communications.

905 Klein, Charna. Counseling Our Own: The Lesbian/Gay Subculture Meets the Mental Health System. Renton, WA: Publication Service, Inc., 1986.

The jacket of the book explains that "This is the first and only book existing on the lesbian/gay counseling service, mental health movement in the United States. It covers how gay counseling services arose from the lesbian/gay subculture and gay movement, why they are needed, their history, organization, philosophy, staff, clients, and relationship with their lesbian/gay communities and the established mental health system."

906 Lindquist, Marie. Holding Back: Why We Hide the Truth About Ourselves. Center City, MN: Hazelden, 1987.

The book explains why people hold back secrets about themselves and then provides a step-by-step plan as to how individuals can take the risks necessary to change.

907 Miranda, Manuel and Harry H.L. Kitano, eds. Mental Health Research and Practice in Minority Communities: Development of Culturally Sensitive Training Programs. Rockville: National Institute of Mental Health, 1986.

Essays in the book include theoretical models for cross-cultural diagnosis and treatment. Ethnic populations mentioned are American Indians, Blacks, Hispanics, Asian Americans, and Pacific Americans.

908 Narcotics Anonymous. 1982; Van Nuys, CA: World Service Office, 1984.

Narcotics Anonymous includes such issues as who is an addict, the Narcotics Anonymous program, how it works, the twelve traditions of NA, recovery, and relapse. The book also includes personal stories of individuals who have recovered through NA. In format, the NA basic text follows the style and is in the spirit and tradition on the AA Big Book.

909 Partners, Box 9685, Seattle, Washington, 98109.

A monthly newsletter for gay and lesbian couples which provides resources, forum space, ideas, and information on building successful relationships.

910 Preston, John and Glenn Swann. Safe Sex: The Ultimate Erotic Guide, The Essential Program of Safe Sexual Practices for Gay Men and Everyone Concerned About AIDS. New York: New American Library, 1986.

Swann shares describes a variety of sexual encounters which are all follow safe sex guidelines.

911 Super Sixty, Box 103, 606 W. Barry, Chicago, IL 60657.

A bi-monthly newsletter for senior gay men seeking lifemates and friends of similar age.

AUTHOR/NAME INDEX

This index includes not only the names of the authors whose work is cited in the NALGAP Annotated Bibliography, but proper names which appear in the citations. For example, "ACOAs and Homosexuality: What's the Connection" (citation 851) is based on an interview with Ellen Ratner. Even though she is not the author of this article, her name is included in this index.

TITLE INDEX

This index includes not only the titles which have been annotated in the NALGAP Annotated Bibliography, but those titles which are mentioned in the annotations. For example, Ian Young's The Male Homosexual in Literature: A Bibliography (citation 765) includes three essays: "The Flower Beneath the Foot: A Short History of the Gay Novel," "The Theatre of Implications: Homosexuality in Drama," and "Ganymede Raped: Gay Literature--The Critic as Censor." Although these essays are not annotated in this bibliography, because they are mentioned in an annotation, they are included in this index.

SUBJECT INDEX

This index includes only those subjects which are found in the annotations. It does not include every issue which is mentioned in each source.